microwave
MUG MEALS

microwave
MUG MEALS

50 delectably tasty home-made dishes – in an instant
... and just a mug to wash up!

THEO MICHAELS

LORENZ BOOKS

CONTENTS

INTRODUCTION

DEDICATED TO MY WIFE AND THREE CHILDREN

Microwave cooking has evolved a lot over the past couple of decades. When I first started researching microwave cooking my mum donated a few of her old microwave cookbooks for me to look at, many of which were promoted as 'Cooking of the Future!' with front covers that resembled a Pink Floyd album more than a cookbook. The recipes in those first cookbooks were impressive: create a whole duck a l'orange in the microwave or an entire roast dinner.

Really?

When microwaves first started appearing in our kitchens they were cutting-edge appliances that were almost positioned as the replacement to conventional cooking, in fact they were sometimes known as electronic ovens. That soon wore off… conventional microwaves don't replace our ovens, but they are exceptional at their very own special type of cooking. There are health as well as speed benefits; microwaves retain more nutrients especially when it comes to cooking vegetables.

The recipes I've created in my cookbook are exactly what I think microwave cooking is all about: quick, healthy dishes packed with flavour!

I want my cookbook to be a loyal microwave companion: make notes, scribble ideas on the page – a good cookbook in my house is covered in splashes, stains and comments; the sign that it is something being used and enjoyed. I hope you enjoy it!

Cooking in the microwave does tend to be more precise than cooking on the hob or in the oven. To help get you on your way there are a few tips and bits of advice that you might find useful. Refer to the manufacturer's instructions for your own microwave.

HOW TO USE THIS BOOK

CHOOSING MUGS:

I've tried to keep every recipe in my book easy, and to use standard mugs that you will have in your cupboard. All the recipes are cooked in a standard 300ml/½ pint mug or a large wide-rimmed 500ml/ 17fl oz mug. If possible always try to choose a wider mug as opposed to tall and thin; a wider mug invariably cooks the meal more evenly and reduces the chances of overspills, whereas tall thin mugs tend to boil over much more easily. Be sure to put your mug on a plate to catch any overspills. Each recipe specifies the minimum size though you can use a larger mug if preferred, or of course, you can cook in any type of microwave-safe bowl or container. Bigger is usually better.

Not everything is suitable to cook in the microwave – any metal containers for instance are a big no-no! (And of course, cutlery should never be microwaved.) If you are unsure whether a mug is microwave-safe just check underneath; most will say on the base whether they can be used in the microwave.

MICROWAVE KNOW-HOW:

Microwaves are now super-sophisticated, many with oven settings, grills and various power settings. However most people I know still end up using just a fraction of the options available. As such, I've avoided any fancy business in my book – all recipes are based on a 800-watt microwave. If you have a microwave with less power then you will need to increase the cooking time – do this in intervals, an extra 30 seconds at a time, taking out the meal to check whether it needs a bit longer.

Remember that all microwaves can still vary slightly: your microwave may be 800W like mine but might in reality be slightly hotter or cooler. You might find that your microwave has certain hot-spots. Equally if you have a rocket-fuelled super-powerful microwave you'll need to reduce the cooking time and again, I would

do this in intervals. If my recipe calls for 2 minutes and your microwave is much more powerful, try a minute first and see if it needs longer. Cooking in the microwave is a bit like seasoning – you can always cook more but you can't cook less. I would always err on the side of increasing the cooking time minimally and then testing it.

All the dishes in the book are cooked uncovered unless specified. When it states that a dish is covered, it is always covered with clear film or plastic wrap and should have a small vent, either a small incision by a knife or the film placed over the mug/bowl with a small gap to one side.

SAFETY FIRST:

The nature of microwave cooking means the ingredients and the vessels can get extremely hot. Always handle with care and use mitts or a cloth to remove vessels from the microwave.

Keep your face away from just-microwaved food, especially for dishes that have been cooked for several minutes or more and that require immediate stirring – they can splash and pop.

When eating microwaved food, sometimes there are pockets of heat within the dish that are hotter than the rest, so please eat slowly, and where the recipe states the dish must stand after cooking – let it stand or it will be hot, hot, hot!

ADAPTING QUANTITIES:

All my recipes are for one person, however, there is nothing stopping you from making two or three mug meals at the same time and putting them in the microwave all at once to cook. You could be the first to have a Microwave Mug Meal party! If you add more than one mug the microwave needs to work harder to cook larger quantities which means you will need to increase your cooking times slightly. If my recipe calls for 2 minutes in the microwave and you are cooking three mugs at once, you will probably need to increase this to 3 or 4 minutes.

Do note that doubling the quantity doesn't mean doubling the cooking time. If you are cooking more than one mug at a time, increase the time by about 15% and see if it needs longer. As an example, if one

mug takes 3 minutes in the microwave, I would microwave two mugs at the same time for about 3 minutes and 45 seconds, see how it looks, then cook longer if needed.

FINALLY:

No recipe is foolproof, whether you are cooking in a conventional oven, under a grill or boiling water on the hob. Ingredients vary in quality, texture, size, density and starting temperature, or might be cut slightly thinner or thicker and take a fraction less or more to cook. Cooking is about having fun, and a little trial and error. Taste the recipe, tweak it to your preferences and feel free to adapt: if I've specified asparagus and you really prefer green beans – then use them!

This is a quick guide to basic staples in the microwave. They are used in some recipes as a base for the dish, and are useful accompaniments to many meals.

SOME EASY BASICS

MASH

Mash is always a great add-on to most meals and is an obvious comfort food, which is good as this couldn't be easier! It also works well with sweet potatoes.

150g/5oz potato, diced
60ml/2fl oz/¼ cup water
7.5ml/1½ tsp butter

90ml/3fl oz/generous ⅓ cup
  milk (optional)
Salt and ground black pepper

Place the potato cubes and the water in a 300ml/½ pint mug or bowl, cover and microwave on full power for 4½ minutes.

Drain the water away. Add the butter and mash the potato with a fork. Add milk to loosen the mash, if liked, and season to taste.

CHEF'S TIP: Add a drizzle of cream for extra indulgence.

PASTA

Pasta cooked in the microwave has been a revelation; its quicker and easier and creates a lot less washing up!

60g/2¼oz dried pasta

300ml/½ pint/1¼ cups hot
  water

Add the pasta and water to a 500ml/17fl oz mug or bowl, ensuring that the pasta is fully submerged. If cooking spaghetti, break it in half. Microwave uncovered on full power for 7 minutes and set aside, leaving it resting in the water. Then drain and use.

RICE

Cooking rice in a large mug is a paradox; it is the simplest recipe to follow yet the hardest to get just right without making a huge mess! Follow my recipe for perfect rice every time that is fluffy and doesn't even need draining. But remember to place the large mug on a plate to catch any overspill.

50g/2oz basmati rice, rinsed

200ml/7fl oz/scant 1 cup water

Place the rice and 150ml/5fl oz/⅔ cup water in a 500ml/17fl oz mug or bowl and microwave uncovered on full power for 5 minutes. Stir and then add the remaining water to the rice. Microwave for a further 5 minutes. Leave to stand for 2 minutes before consuming.

CHEF'S TIP: If you start to stir the cooked rice with a spoon it will go mushy and sticky; instead gently stab with a fork to keep it fluffy.

PASTRY

Who knew you could cook pastry in the microwave! This is basically a standard shortcrust pastry recipe which works surprisingly well.

30ml/2 tbsp plain/all-purpose flour

15ml/1 tbsp butter

Pinch salt

2.5ml/½ tsp water

Pinch of turmeric

Mix all the ingredients together in a mug or bowl with a spoon until incorporated, it will be a bit sticky. Using both hands roll the sticky dough into a ball, cover and leave to rest for 10 minutes.

When ready place the ball on a floured work surface and flatten by hand to about 1cm/½in thick. Place on a lightly dusted plate and microwave for 1 minute, checking after 30 seconds. Leave to stand and don't touch!

Carefully lift the pastry from the plate and place on top of your chosen mug meal.

CHEF'S TIP: The turmeric is purely to give your pastry that golden colour you get from baking in the oven, it won't taste.

INSTANT IDEAS FOR BREAKFAST

They say breakfast is the most important meal of the day, it gives you the energy you need and kick-starts your metabolism. I've created a few breakfast recipes based on what I love to eat (yes, there is a fry-up, even though I'm racked with guilt after eating one!) but there are also a couple of real surprises showing what you can create using the microwave. My Magic Eggs Florentine is the reverse engineering of a Hollandaise sauce that is traditionally a finicky recipe to get right, but now works perfectly every time!

I think everyone should be able to enjoy a good breakfast all day, and this one is no exception! All the traditional items found in a fry-up but with a fraction of the amount of oil. Made fast and enjoyed slow for a lazy duvet day.

ALL-DAY BREAKFAST

SERVES 1
COOKING TIME: 6 minutes 20 seconds (800W microwave)
EQUIPMENT: 300ml/½ pint mug, small plates

2 slices tomato, width of a finger thickness

30ml/2 tbsp olive oil
2 rashers/strips streaky/ fatty bacon
50g/2oz potato
1 egg
15ml/1 tbsp milk
5ml/1 tsp mayonnaise
Pinch salt and ground black pepper

1 Place the tomato slices in the mug, drizzle over half the oil and microwave on full power for 1½ minutes. Take out the tomato and reserve on a small plate.

2 Line the mug with the bacon rashers in a 'U' shape, and microwave on full power for 2 minutes. Take out the bacon and reserve on a separate plate, it will continue to crisp after cooking.

3 Grate the potato and give it a gentle squeeze to remove some of the excess liquid. Place in the mug, pour in the remaining oil with a pinch of salt and pepper. Cover and microwave for 2 minutes.

4 Add the egg and milk to the cooked potato and whisk with a fork until fully incorporated. Cover and microwave for 30 seconds. Remove from the microwave and stir. Microwave for 20 further seconds and then stir again.

5 Break the bacon into small pieces and add to the mixture. Add the secret ingredient (that's the mayonnaise!) and mix well, place the cooked tomatoes on top, sit down, put your feet up and enjoy.

Mexican in origin and now a popular dish worldwide; whenever I hear the words Huevos Rancheros it always brings to mind an image of a dusky morning with a couple of cowboys cooking breakfast on a shovel over an open fire. I sometimes tear the bread and pop on top of the mug.

RAPIDO HUEVOS RANCHEROS

1 Add all the ingredients for the sauce into the mug, reserving 15ml/1 tbsp olive oil for later. Cover and microwave on full power for 6 minutes, giving it a quick stir after 3 minutes. After 6 minutes the watery tomato sauce will be transformed into a thick mixture. Handle the mug with care as it will be very hot!

2 Add the spinach and half the coriander to the sauce and combine well.

3 Using the back of a spoon, gently flatten the top of the sauce, crack the egg on top and drizzle over the remaining olive oil. Cover and microwave for 2 minutes (if you are using a small egg or for a runnier yolk check after 90 seconds).

4 Garnish with the remaining coriander and the chilli slices, and serve with bread.

CHEF'S TIPS:
Depending on how smoky the chipotle paste is you can add 2.5ml/½ tsp of smoked paprika to the sauce, or to taste.

Chipotle paste is usually quite fiery but add a splash of chilli sauce or more chilli slices if you want more bite to your breakfast!

Try adding a dollop of yogurt to counterbalance the heat of the chilli.

SERVES 1
COOKING TIME: **8 minutes** (800W microwave)
EQUIPMENT: **500ml/17fl oz mug**

25g/1oz spinach, roughly chopped
30ml/2 tbsp chopped fresh coriander/cilantro
1 egg
Few slices green jalapeño chilli
½ slice bread, to serve

For the sauce:
50g/2oz bell pepper, diced (any colour!)
20g/¼oz diced onion
1 clove garlic, chopped
120ml/4fl oz/½ cup canned chopped tomatoes
15ml/1 tbsp dried oregano
5ml/1 tsp chipotle paste
30ml/2 tbsp olive oil

Not strictly a microwave mug meal, but a fantastic way of using a microwave for a delicious bite to eat. The Hollandaise sauce is a triumph of a classic recipe often fraught with danger but which can be done perfectly in the microwave every time.

MAGIC EGGS FLORENTINE

SERVES 1
COOKING TIME: 3 minutes
**   45 seconds (800W**
**   microwave)**
EQUIPMENT: 2 x 500ml/
**   17fl oz mugs, bowl, plate**

6 fresh baby spinach leaves
1 toasted and buttered
    English muffin
Salt and ground black
    pepper
Chives, chopped, and a pinch
    cayenne pepper, to garnish

For the hollandaise sauce:
1 egg yolk
60g/2¼oz butter
15ml/1 tbsp water
7.5ml/1½ tsp vinegar
Pinch salt

For the poached egg:
1 medium/US large egg,
    at room temperature
75ml/2½fl oz/⅓ cup water,
    or just enough to cover
    the egg
2.5ml/½ tsp butter (optional)

CHEF'S TIP:
Add a rasher/strip of cooked streaky/fatty bacon or ham on top of the spinach for a meatier meal. To cook bacon rashers simply microwave on full power (800W microwave) on a small plate uncovered for 2 minutes or slightly longer if you like it extra-crispy.

1 To make the hollandaise, add the egg yolk to a mug or bowl, gently whisk to break the yolk and set aside. Place all the other ingredients into a separate mug and microwave uncovered on full power for 3 minutes. Once done, immediately (you need to act quick with this one!) start to drizzle the butter sauce into the egg yolk, whisking all the time until fully incorporated. By now you will have a rich silky hollandaise sauce. If you want to loosen the mixture just add a tiny splash of tepid water to the sauce.

2 For the poached egg, gently crack the egg into a large mug and pour in water and butter, if using. Microwave uncovered on full power for 45 seconds.

3 Layer the spinach leaves over the toasted muffin on a serving plate. Gently place the drained poached egg on top of the spinach.

4 Pour the hollandaise sauce over the poached egg. Season to taste and garnish with chives and cayenne pepper. Smile, with justified pride, and enjoy.

Everyone loves pizza, everyone loves muffins – so here's the perfect combination of both! You can serve it with a side of rocket and cherry tomatoes for a brunch dish. The other great thing about this recipe is you can have fun with different toppings; try adding some olives, pepperoni, or extra cheese.

PUFFIN IN A MUG

SERVES 1
COOKING TIME: 1½ minutes
   (800W microwave), plus
   1 minute standing
EQUIPMENT: 300ml/½ pint
   mug

1 small/US medium egg
15ml/1 tbsp olive oil
30ml/2 tbsp milk
Pinch ground black pepper
60ml/4 tbsp plain/all-purpose
   flour
5ml/1 tsp baking powder
10g/¼oz grated Parmesan
   cheese
10g/¼oz baby plum
   tomatoes, quartered
1 anchovy fillet, sliced
2.5ml/½ tsp dried oregano
10g/¼oz grated Cheddar
   cheese

1 Place the egg, olive oil and milk in the mug and whisk together.

2 Then add all the other ingredients except the Cheddar cheese and stir to combine.

3 Sprinkle the Cheddar cheese on top and microwave uncovered on full power for 1½ minutes.

4 Leave to stand for 1 minute before eating.

CHEF'S TIPS:
If you don't have Parmesan cheese you can substitute with additional Cheddar to mix through the muffin which will also make it slightly more moist.

Try garnishing the top of the muffin before cooking with a sprinkle of anchovies or a few slices of tomato.

MAINLY MEAT

I'm such a carnivore and was excited to create some delicious meals in the microwave that would satisfy my caveman fix in a few minutes. After experimenting I found certain meats work really well in the microwave. White meats such as pork and chicken keep their succulence especially when cooked in liquid or wrapped in pancetta or bacon. Red meats tend to get tough very quickly if over-cooked, but I've found the secret is to use the residual heat of liquids; in the Beef Stifado, the sauce continues to cook the thinly sliced steak perfectly and keeps it tender. There are some real microwave meal stars in this chapter which I hope you enjoy as much as I do!

What can one say about a Spaghetti Bolognese that hasn't been said already? This version is done in 10 minutes and tastes amazing! If you fancy a quick Italian meal my microwaved bolognese sauce is perfect, and tastes as if it has been slow cooking for hours.

SPEEDY SPAGHETTI BOLOGNESE

SERVES 1
COOKING TIME: 3 minutes (800W microwave), plus 7 minutes standing
EQUIPMENT: 500ml/17fl oz mug, 300ml/½ pint mug

60g/2¼oz dried spaghetti, broken in half
300ml/½ pint/1¼ cups hot water
Salt and ground black pepper
15ml/1 tbsp grated Parmesan cheese

For the bolognese sauce:
15ml/1 tbsp olive oil
25g/1oz onion, grated
1 clove garlic, finely chopped or grated
4 cherry tomatoes, halved
15ml/1 tbsp tomato purée/paste
65g/½oz minced/ground beef
5ml/1 tsp dried oregano
15ml/1 tbsp water

1 Add your spaghetti to the larger 500ml/17fl oz mug or bowl with the water and microwave on full power uncovered for 7 minutes and reserve, leaving it resting in the water.

2 Add all the ingredients for the bolognese sauce to the smaller mug, stir well, cover with clear film or plastic wrap (leaving a vent) and microwave on full power for 3 minutes.

3 Drain the spaghetti, add to the bolognese sauce and combine well. Season to taste and garnish with gratings of Parmesan cheese.

CHEF'S TIPS:
Top with some chopped fresh parsley, if liked.
Try adding a hint of spice with 5ml/1 tsp of ground cinnamon to the bolognese sauce before cooking.

Sitting at a street stall in Ho Chi Min and diving into a steaming bowl of beef pho (pronounced 'fuh') is one of life's great pleasures. Beef or chicken pho is available on every street corner of Vietnam and the hawkers spend hours perfecting their pho, which can take over 24 hours to cook. This version is ready in minutes.

VIETNAMESE-STYLE BEEF PHO

1 Place the dried rice noodles into the mug; you may need to break them up to fit. Pour over the boiling water until it reaches the same height as the noodles, cover the mug and leave to stand for 5 minutes. Drain, leaving the noodles and roughly 15ml/1 tbsp of the water in the mug.

2 Add the garlic, ginger and vegetable oil to the noodles, stir and microwave on full power for 1 minute.

3 Now add the chicken stock, sugar, sesame oil, soy sauce, fish sauce, beansprouts and pak choi and microwave again for 1 minute.

4 Gently stir and then place the thinly sliced steak over the top and gently submerge into the cooking water with a fork. The residual heat of the soup will cook the steak through, as it is traditionally served on the streets of Ho Chi Min.

5 Garnish with chilli slices, fresh coriander, mint leaves, spring onion and lime juice.

CHEF'S TIPS:

For a more economical version try using rump instead of sirloin steak or even chicken, but pre-cook the chicken first by submerging in water and microwave on full power for 3 minutes or until cooked through.

Turn this into a vegetarian dish by using vegetable stock instead of chicken and substituting baby aubergines/eggplants for the meat.

If you can find Thai basil include a few leaves for a really distinctive flavour.

SERVES 1
COOKING TIME: **2 minutes (800W microwave), plus 5 minutes standing**
EQUIPMENT: **500ml/17fl oz mug**

60g/2¼oz dried rice noodles
300ml/½ pint/1¼ cups boiling water
1 clove garlic, grated
1cm/½in fresh root ginger, grated
7.5ml/1½ tsp vegetable oil
150ml/¼ pint/⅔ cup chicken stock, warm
2.5ml/½ tsp soft light brown sugar
5ml/1 tsp sesame oil
5ml/1 tsp light soy sauce
5ml/1 tsp fish sauce
30ml/2 tbsp beansprouts
1 whole pak choi/bok choy, roughly chopped
35g/1⅓oz sirloin steak, sliced very thin, at room temperature
½ red chilli, thinly sliced
15ml/1 tbsp chopped fresh coriander/cilantro
15ml/1 tbsp fresh mint leaves, torn
½ spring onion/scallion, finely sliced
Squeeze lime juice

Everyone loves a great Chilli con Carne and this one is no exception. Recipes vary from the quick and easy to gourmet meals that are slow-cooked for hours. My version doesn't take hours to cook, in fact you're done in under 10 minutes! And I've added a little secret ingredient to really 'beef' up the flavour.

CHILLI CON CARNE WITH RICE

SERVES 1
COOKING TIME: 9 minutes (800W microwave), plus 3 minutes standing
EQUIPMENT: 500ml/17fl oz mug

25g/1oz onion, grated
1 clove garlic, grated
65g/2½oz minced/ground beef
5ml/1 tsp dried oregano
15ml/1 tbsp tomato purée/paste
5ml/1 tsp ground cumin
5ml/1 tsp smoked paprika
5ml/1 tsp ground chilli powder, hot or mild to taste
20g/¾oz basmati rice
200ml/7fl oz/scant 1 cup beef stock
15ml/1 tbsp olive oil
100g/3¾oz canned kidney beans, drained and rinsed
15ml/1 tbsp instant gravy granules
5ml/1 tsp natural/plain yogurt
15ml/1 tbsp chopped fresh coriander/cilantro
Salt and ground black pepper

1 Place the onion, garlic, beef, oregano, tomato purée, all the spices, rice, half the stock and the olive oil in the mug and mix thoroughly to break up the meat. Cover and microwave on full power for 5 minutes.

2 Remove from the microwave, stir well and add the remaining beef stock and kidney beans. Microwave again covered for 2½ minutes.

3 Remove from the microwave, stir again and add the gravy granules. Mix thoroughly then cover and microwave for 1½ minutes. Leave to stand for 3 minutes.

4 Serve garnished with a dollop of yogurt and fresh coriander and seasoned to taste.

CHEF'S TIPS:
The gravy granules give a nice thickness to the dish as well as extra beef flavour.
   Always make a bit more stock than the recipe calls for so you can add a little more to loosen the dish if it's too thick.
   If you want to make this dish really hot add a pinch of dried chilli flakes at the start, alternatively if you're looking for a quick kid's lunch you can leave out the chilli altogether!

The famous Greek stew, usually cooked over several hours, now redesigned for your (almost) instant gratification. Stifado means a Greek stew that is cooked with lots and lots of onions, usually whole baby or pearl onions or shallots.

FUSS-FREE BEEF STIFADO

SERVES 1
COOKING TIME: 7½ minutes (800W microwave), plus 3 minutes standing
EQUIPMENT: 300ml/½ pint mug

70g/2¾oz onions, thinly sliced
1 clove garlic, thinly sliced
60ml/4 tbsp olive oil
Good pinch salt and ground black pepper

15ml/1 tbsp tomato purée/paste
2.5ml/½ tsp ground cinnamon
1 stick cinnamon, about 5cm/2in in length
100g/3¾oz canned butter/lima beans, drained and rinsed
50ml/2fl oz/¼ cup beef stock
7.5ml/1½ tsp malt vinegar
80g/3¼oz rump steak, very thinly sliced
Sprig fresh parsley

1 Place the onions, garlic, 45ml/3 tbsp of the olive oil and a good pinch of salt and ground black pepper in the mug and microwave uncovered on full power for 4 minutes.

2 Stir well and then add the tomato purée, cinnamon (ground and stick), butter beans and the stock and microwave again, covered, for 3 minutes.

3 Stir well and finally add the vinegar, remaining 15ml/1 tbsp olive oil, and the steak slices. Add a splash of water or stock at this stage if the mixture is too thick. Microwave on full power for 30 seconds, leave to stand for 3 minutes and serve garnished with a sprig of fresh parsley.

CHEF'S TIP:
Use the steak at room temperature as it is predominantly cooked in the residual heat of the stew. This ensures that the meat is really tender but is still cooked through.

The magic of the microwave... stuffed peppers are a great recipe to have in your repertoire but usually take ages to make. This is one of those dishes where cooking in the microwave really comes into its own. This is done in two super-easy stages, and can be cooked in under 10 minutes.

STUFFED RED PEPPER WITH FETA CHEESE

SERVES 1
COOKING TIME: 8–9 minutes
(800W microwave)
EQUIPMENT: 500ml/17fl oz
mug, bowl

1 bell pepper
3 asparagus, finely sliced
½ clove garlic, finely diced
30g/1¼oz minced/ground beef
15ml/1 tbsp tomato purée/paste
7.5ml/1½ tsp olive oil
Small pinch chilli flakes

45ml/3 tbsp water
15ml/1 tbsp couscous
25g/1oz courgette/ zucchini, diced
15ml/1 tbsp chopped fresh parsley
15ml/1 tbsp chopped fresh coriander/cilantro
15ml/1 tbsp chopped fresh spinach leaves
35g/1⅓oz cherry tomatoes, diced
30g/1¼oz feta cheese
Salt and ground black pepper

1 Prepare your pepper by cutting the very top off so you have a wide opening. Remove the seeds and stem from inside.

2 Place 15ml/1 tbsp water in the bottom of the mug and then put the pepper in the mug; the water will help steam the outside of the pepper.

3 Thoroughly mix the remaining water and all the other ingredients, except the feta cheese and seasoning, together in a bowl. Stuff the pepper with the mixture, pushing it down with the back of a spoon.

4 Cover the mug and microwave on full power for 8 minutes. Be careful of the steam when you remove the cover. Check the flesh of the pepper – you want it quite soft but with some texture. If it feels hard to the touch then microwave for another minute – this may vary depending on the size of your pepper.

5 Serve topped with crumbled feta cheese, season to taste and enjoy!

This fragrant north African stew is named after the vessel it is cooked in, the tagine. Famous for its depth of flavour and combination of fruit, nuts and spices, enjoy your own mug version cooked in a matter of minutes opposed to hours. This is a really good dish to use up leftover roast lamb!

LAMB 'TAGINE' IN A MUG

SERVES 1

COOKING TIME: 8 minutes
(800W microwave), plus
2 minutes standing

EQUIPMENT: 500ml/17fl oz
mug

20g/¾oz onion, grated
1 clove garlic, grated
2.5ml/½ tsp ground cumin
2.5ml/½ tsp smoked paprika
2.5ml/½ tsp ground
    cinnamon
15ml/1 tbsp tomato
    purée/paste
45ml/3 tbsp olive oil
50g/2oz aubergine/
    eggplant, diced
85ml/3fl oz/generous
    ⅓ cup lamb stock

100g/3¾oz canned chickpeas,
    drained and rinsed
25g/1oz dried dates, pitted
    and sliced into thirds
15ml/1 tbsp flaked/sliced
    almonds, plus a few extra
    for garnish
80g/3¼oz lamb chump
    steak, cut into small
    bitesize cubes
Sprigs fresh coriander/
    cilantro
Few pomegranate seeds
Salt and ground black
    pepper

1 Place the onion, garlic, all the spices, tomato purée, two-thirds of the olive oil, the aubergine and about a quarter of the stock in the mug and microwave uncovered on full power for 3 minutes.

2 Remove from the microwave, stir well and then add the chickpeas, the remaining stock and season with salt and ground black pepper. Cover and microwave again for 4 minutes.

3 Remove from the microwave and stir in the dates and almonds. Place the lamb gently on top of the stew, drizzle over the rest of the olive oil and season the lamb heavily. Microwave for 1 minute and then fold the lamb into the rest of the stew. The lamb will still be a little pink which is how I would normally serve this cut of meat; once combined with the rest of the tagine it will cook through. Leave the tagine to stand for 2 minutes.

4 Serve garnished with a few extra almonds, fresh coriander sprigs and a few pomegranate seeds.

CHEF'S TIPS:
Microwave cooking doesn't like sinew or fats in meat very much, they go tough. Try to cut off any connective tissue or fat from the lamb.

For a vegetarian version simply replace the quantity of lamb with double the amount of aubergine/ eggplant, adding it with the rest of the ingredients at the beginning.

A great new twist on a classic favourite; my Caribbean shepherd's pie. All the usual suspects but with a nod to the flavours of the Caribbean: a rich meat sauce with the fruity heat of Scotch bonnet chilli, fluffy buttery sweet potato mash, and the aromatics of allspice running through the dish.

'GET YOUR JERK ON' SHEPHERD'S PIE

SERVES 1
COOKING TIME: 10½ minutes
   (800W microwave), plus
   1 minute standing
EQUIPMENT: 300ml/½ pint
   mug, bowl

150g/5oz sweet potato,
   peeled and diced
90ml/3fl oz/⅓ cup water
7.5ml/1½ tsp butter
15g/½oz onion, diced
1 clove garlic, chopped
15ml/1 tbsp olive oil
1 spring onion/scallion,
   roughly sliced
20g/¾oz carrot, diced
¼ Scotch bonnet chilli,
   roughly chopped (see
   chef's tip below!)

60g/2¼oz minced/ground
   lamb
50g/2oz frozen peas
2.5ml/½ tsp dried thyme
2.5ml/½ tsp ground allspice
5ml/1 tsp soft light brown
   sugar
5ml/1 tsp malt vinegar
5ml/1 tsp tomato
   purée/paste
2.5ml/½ tsp ground
   cinnamon
15ml/1 tbsp gravy granules
30ml/2 tbsp water
5ml/1 tsp chopped fresh
   mint leaves
Salt and ground black
   pepper

1 Start by making the sweet potato mash: place the sweet potato and water together in a bowl, cover and microwave on full power for 4½ minutes. Drain, add the butter and mash with a fork. Set aside.

2 Place the onion, garlic, olive oil, spring onion, carrot and chilli into the mug and microwave uncovered on full power for 3 minutes.

3 Add the lamb to the mug and mix well. Then add all the remaining ingredients, except the mint and seasoning, to the mug. Microwave uncovered on full power for a further 3 minutes.

4 Remove from the microwave, stir well and leave to stand for 1 minute. Stir in the fresh mint and scoop the sweet potato mash on top. Season to taste and serve.

CHEF'S TIP:
Scotch bonnet chillies are hot! If you want a milder version use a jalapeño chilli instead. If using a Scotch bonnet please wear gloves or try to only touch the outside skin, not the part you have cut. Wash your hands thoroughly after handling them.

This just looks awesome! A famous Greek recipe that is cooked in less than ten minutes and has all the criteria of an authentic moussaka: creamy béchamel sauce, layers of aubergine and a rich meat sauce that fills the kitchen with the scent of cinnamon and the dream of sitting in a Greek taverna on the beach.

TOWERING MOUSSAKA

SERVES 1
COOKING TIME: 7 minutes
(800W microwave)
EQUIPMENT: bowls, 300ml/
½ pint mug

15g/½oz onion, diced
1 clove garlic, finely diced
5ml/1 tsp dried oregano
5ml/1 tsp ground cinnamon
7.5ml/1½ tsp tomato ketchup
70g/2¾oz minced/ground
    lamb
30ml/2 tbsp chopped fresh
    parsley, plus extra
    to garnish

7.5ml/1½ tsp olive oil,
    plus a few extra drops
    for greasing
3 discs of aubergine/
    eggplant, cut widthways
    about 2.5cm/1in thick

For the béchamel sauce:
15ml/1 tbsp butter
15ml/1 tbsp plain/
    all-purpose flour
100ml/3½fl oz/scant ½ cup
    milk
50g/2oz grated Cheddar
    cheese (use mature/sharp
    for extra cheesy flavour!)
Salt and ground black
    pepper

1 Combine all the ingredients together for the moussaka except the aubergine in a bowl, and mix.

2 Place a few drops of olive oil in the bottom of the mug, then place one disc of aubergine so it lies flat on the bottom (trim it slightly if it doesn't fit, but it's alright for it to be a bit snug).

3 Add half the meat mixture on top of the aubergine, pressing it down gently, then another disc of aubergine, then the remaining meat and finally the third disc of aubergine.

4 Microwave uncovered on full power for 5 minutes and then leave to stand in the mug while you prepare the béchamel sauce.

5 Melt the butter in a bowl in the microwave for 30 seconds, add the flour and mix thoroughly. Slowly pour over 25ml/1fl oz/⅛ cup milk and mix to a paste with a fork before adding the remaining milk. Don't worry if it is a lumpy, sticky mess, it gets better.

6 Microwave uncovered on full power for 30 seconds, remove and whisk thoroughly with a fork. Microwave again for 1 minute. Remove from the microwave and stir in the cheese and seasoning to taste. Pour the béchamel sauce over the top of the moussaka and garnish with fresh parsley.

CHEF'S TIP:
Want to really see this in all its glory? Before you add the béchamel sauce place a serving plate face-down on top of the mug. Flip them over, give it a gentle shake and slowly lift the mug to reveal your moussaka. Then drizzle the béchamel sauce over the top.

There is something about lamb and coconut that just goes together so well; add to that some crunch, a bit of spice and you have a mug of soul food to curl up around and enjoy. Satay is usually dry, so my version adds a bit more sauce to give the rice noodles something to be smothered in.

LAMB SATAY CURRY

SERVES 1
COOKING TIME: 4½ minutes (800W microwave), plus 3 minutes standing
EQUIPMENT: 300ml/½ pint mug

25g/1oz dried rice noodles, medium width
200ml/7fl oz/scant 1 cup water, just boiled
20g/¾oz onion, finely sliced
1 clove garlic, finely sliced
20g/¾oz beansprouts
40g/1½oz runner/green beans, thinly sliced
2.5ml/½ tsp sesame oil

10ml/2 tsp vegetable oil
70g/2¾oz lamb steak, finely sliced
Dozen Thai basil leaves, torn
5ml/1 tsp chopped peanuts, to garnish
Salt and ground black pepper

For the satay sauce:
100ml/3½fl oz/scant ½ cup coconut milk
30ml/2 tbsp peanut butter
2.5ml/½ tsp dark soy sauce
5ml/1 tsp fish sauce
2.5ml/½ tsp sugar

1 Add the rice noodles and just-boiled water to the mug. There is no set time to soak the noodles as they will cook later in the recipe, so while the noodles are soaking prepare the rest of the ingredients.

2 Drain the noodles, leaving a few drops of water inside the mug. Add the onion, garlic, beansprouts, runner beans, sesame oil and 7.5ml/1½ tsp of the vegetable oil and stir into the noodles. Microwave uncovered on full power for 2 minutes.

3 Add all the ingredients for the satay sauce to the mug with the noodles and combine, then rest the lamb on top (don't mix the lamb into the dish). Drizzle with the remaining 2.5ml/½ tsp vegetable oil and season. Microwave for 1½ minutes, stir, then microwave again for 1 minute.

4 Leave to stand for 3 minutes, stir the torn basil leaves through and then serve garnished with a scattering of chopped peanuts.

CHEF'S TIP:
I like using crunchy peanut butter as I enjoy the little bits of peanuts you get, but smooth will work just as well!

This delicious dish is inspired by a recipe my mum cooks with lamb and lots of lemon juice and oregano which creates this divine yet humble stew. If you really fancy a pie, simply add a crispy pastry top – see my recipe on page 11, it only takes another couple of minutes!

LEMON AND OREGANO LAMB STEW

SERVES 1
COOKING TIME: 7½ minutes
(800W microwave)
EQUIPMENT: 300ml/½ pint
mug

30g/1¼oz potato, diced into
small cubes
30g/1¼oz onion, grated
2 chestnut mushrooms,
chopped
1 clove garlic, grated
30ml/2 tbsp olive oil

Pinch sugar
15ml/1 tbsp dried oregano
50ml/2fl oz/¼ cup stock,
ideally lamb but chicken
or beef if not
30ml/2 tbsp frozen peas
100g/3¾oz minced/ground
lamb
22.5ml/1½ tbsp plain/
all-purpose flour
15ml/1 tbsp lemon juice
Salt and ground black
pepper

1 Place the potato, onion, mushrooms, garlic and 15ml/1 tbsp olive oil in the mug and microwave uncovered on full power for 4½ minutes.

2 Remove from the microwave and stir well. Add the sugar, oregano, stock, peas, lamb and flour and mix thoroughly until all combined. Microwave again uncovered on full power for 3 minutes.

3 Stir in the lemon juice and if the stew appears too thick add a little water. Serve seasoned with salt and ground black pepper to taste.

CHEF'S TIP:
If you want a more traditional mint and lamb stew, simply swap in mint instead of oregano and malt vinegar instead of lemon juice.

Feijoada is the ultimate Brazilian soul food, the black beans give this dish a lovely depth of flavour and seductive tanned look – the sort of tan you can only get on Ipanema beach! It tastes great for supper and even better after a night of caipirinhas and trying to dance the samba!

FEIJOADA – BRAZILIAN BLACK BEAN STEW

SERVES 1
COOKING TIME: 5½ minutes (800W microwave), plus 3 minutes standing
EQUIPMENT: 300ml/½ pint mug

60g/2¼oz skinless pork belly, diced into bitesize cubes
1 rasher/strip streaky/ fatty smoked bacon, roughly chopped
30ml/2 tbsp olive oil
15g/½oz onion, grated
1 clove garlic, grated
5ml/1 tsp tomato purée/paste
1 sprig of thyme, plus extra to garnish
2.5ml/½ tsp smoked paprika
180g/6¼oz canned black beans, (about ½ can) drained
15ml/1 tbsp water
Salt and ground black pepper

1 Place the pork belly, bacon and half the olive oil in the mug and season with a pinch of salt and ground black pepper. Microwave uncovered on full power for 1½ minutes. Remove from the microwave and drain some of the juices from the mug.

2 Add the grated onion, garlic, tomato purée, thyme, paprika and the rest of the olive oil. Microwave covered on full power for 1 minute.

3 Add the black beans and water and microwave covered for 1½ minutes. Remove, stir and microwave again for a further 1½ minutes uncovered.

4 Mix well and leave to stand for 3 minutes. Serve garnished with some extra thyme.

CHEF'S TIP:
You can also add a dollop of yogurt at the end for extra garnish.

Louisiana is a state that captures the imagination; it is steeped in history as a melting pot of French, African and American cultures. Bring some of that New Orleans Mardi Gras back home with a mug of gumbo. This looks like a lot of ingredients but it's big-easy to make and delicious to eat!

THE BIG EASY — LOUISIANA GUMBO

1 Put the flour and vegetable oil in the mug and mix well to combine, then add the paprika and season with salt and ground black pepper. Microwave uncovered on full power for 2 minutes.

2 Add the bacon, celery, onion, garlic, pepper, okra, thyme and half the stock, and mix the ingredients as much as possible; the bacon will stick together but separates later during cooking. Microwave covered on full power for 4 minutes.

SERVES 1
**COOKING TIME: 5 minutes
(800W microwave), plus
2 minutes standing**
**EQUIPMENT: 500ml/17fl oz
mug**

30ml/2 tbsp flour
30ml/2 tbsp vegetable oil
5ml/1 tsp paprika
1 rasher/strip streaky/
  fatty bacon, diced
15g/½oz celery, finely diced
20g/¾oz onion, grated
1 clove garlic, grated
15g/½oz green bell pepper,
  finely diced
4 okra, sliced roughly
  2.5cm/1in thick

1 sprig fresh thyme
180ml/6fl oz/⅓ cup chicken
  stock
40g/1½oz smoked or garlic
  sausage, roughly diced
5 king prawns/jumbo shrimp
30g/1¼oz/2–3 baby plum
  tomatoes, diced
5ml/1 tsp Dijon mustard
2.5ml/½ tsp hot sauce
15ml/1 tbsp chopped fresh
  parsley
15ml/1 tbsp lemon juice
Drizzle olive oil
Salt and ground black
  pepper

3 Add the sausage, prawns, tomatoes, mustard, hot sauce and the remaining stock, and microwave covered for a further 3 minutes.

4 Add the parsley and lemon juice and stir through. Leave to stand for 2 minutes and then serve garnished with a drizzle of olive oil.

CHEF'S TIP:
If you like your food hot use picante paprika or add a pinch of cayenne pepper at the start!

Hong Kong is a city of extremes, the calm and chaotic, the old and new, but one thing is consistent: if it's food and you can buy it on the street it will be good. This dish pays homage to the delicious clay hotpots in Kowloon that are loved by tourists and locals alike. Pork is a very popular ingredient.

HONG KONG CLAY HOTPOT RICE

SERVES 1
COOKING TIME: 10½ minutes (800W microwave), plus 2 minutes standing
EQUIPMENT: 500ml/17fl oz mug, small bowl

40g/1½oz basmati rice, rinsed well
160ml/5½fl oz/⅔ cup tepid water
100g/3¾oz pork belly, cut into bitesize cubes
5ml/1 tsp fresh root ginger, finely sliced
½ clove garlic, finely sliced
60g/2¼oz aubergine/ eggplant, cut into width strips
5ml/1 tsp sesame oil
15ml/1 tbsp olive oil
Fresh coriander/cilantro leaves, to garnish
Salt and ground black pepper

For the sauce:
15ml/1 tbsp light soy sauce
Pinch sugar
Pinch Chinese five spice powder
2 spring onions/scallions, sliced
½ red chilli, sliced

1 Place the basmati rice and 100ml/3.5fl oz/scant ½ cup of the water in the mug. Microwave covered on full power for 3 minutes.

2 Gently push the pork belly into the rice, add 30ml/ 1fl oz/⅛ cup more water and microwave again, covered, for 3 minutes.

3 Add the ginger, garlic, aubergine, oils and the remaining 30ml/1fl oz/⅛ cup water and microwave covered for a further 3 minutes.

4 Combine all of the sauce ingredients in a small bowl and then spoon over the top of the rice. Cover again and microwave for a final 90 seconds. Remove from the microwave, stir through and leave to stand for 2 minutes.

5 Season to taste, serve garnished with fresh coriander leaves and enjoy!

CHEF'S TIPS:
Make sure you sit the mug on a small plate whilst in the microwave to catch any overflow.
You can replace the pork with pak choi/bok choy and broad/fava beans for a vegetarian version.

After travelling through Laos for a few weeks I eventually found myself in Vang Vieng, a tourist hotspot, and had my first plate of Laap. Laap is the national dish of Laos and is in essence a meat salad dish. The meat is fried and given an additionally intense flavour with fish sauce. It is a really healthy and vibrant-tasting recipe.

LAAP — A LAOS NATIONAL DISH

SERVES 1
COOKING TIME: 1½ minutes (800W microwave), plus 1 minute standing
EQUIPMENT: 300ml/½ pint mug

10g/¼oz vermicelli glass noodles, broken into 2.5cm/1in pieces
80g/3¼oz minced/ground pork
15ml/1 tbsp oil
5ml/1 tsp cornflour/cornstarch
20g/¾oz beansprouts
½ red chilli, chopped and not deseeded, or 2.5ml/½ tsp dried chilli flakes
15ml/1 tbsp nam pla (fish sauce)
15ml/1 tbsp lime juice
Pinch sugar
30ml/2 tbsp torn fresh Thai basil leaves
30ml/2 tbsp torn fresh coriander/cilantro leaves
30ml/2 tbsp torn fresh mint leaves
6 torn fresh spinach leaves
Salt and ground black pepper

1 Place the noodles in the bottom of the mug, then add the pork, oil, cornflour and seasoning and lightly mix with a fork (the noodles won't combine at this stage but it's fine for them to remain at the bottom of the mug).

2 Place the beansprouts on top and microwave uncovered on full power for 1½ minutes.

3 Remove from the microwave, break up the meat with a fork and combine with the noodles and beansprouts.

4 Add the remaining ingredients to the mug, stir well and leave to stand for 1 minute. Season to taste and serve immediately.

CHEF'S TIPS:
If you want some extra crunch add a few chopped peanuts at the end.

Laap isn't exclusively made with pork, you can use chicken, beef or even fish. The one I had in Laos was made with pork so I've stuck with tradition!

The secret of a good dhal is all in the final addition of the tempered spices and the ghee or butter. I use pork belly in this version to make it a meal in its own right. Don't be put off by its appearance during the cooking process, it all comes together at the very end!

PORK BELLY DHAL

SERVES 1
COOKING TIME: **9 minutes**
   (800W microwave)
EQUIPMENT: **500ml/17fl oz**
   mug, small bowl

50g/2oz dried red split lentils,
   rinsed thoroughly
150ml/¼ pint/⅔ cup water
65g/2½oz pork belly, diced
   into bitesize pieces
20g/¾oz okra or asparagus,
   roughly sliced
Sprigs fresh coriander/
   cilantro, to garnish

For the spice paste:
15ml/1 tbsp butter
2.5ml/½ tsp olive oil
1.5ml/¼ tsp garam masala
1.5ml/¼ tsp turmeric
1.5ml/¼ tsp nigella seeds
1.5ml/¼ tsp ground cumin
1.5ml/¼ tsp chilli powder
10g/¼oz onion, finely
   chopped
5ml/1 tsp fresh root ginger,
   grated
1.5ml/¼ tsp salt

1 Place the red lentils and 125ml/4fl oz/½ cup of the water in the mug and microwave uncovered on full power for 4 minutes. Remove from the microwave and skim any foam from the surface of the cooking water.

2 Add the pork belly, okra or asparagus and remaining 25ml/1fl oz/⅛ cup water to the mug. Cover and microwave on full power for 3½ minutes.

3 Remove from the microwave and stir thoroughly to help break up the lentils, adding a drop more water if the mixture is too thick, and then set the mug aside to stand.

4 In a small bowl add all the spice paste ingredients and microwave uncovered on full power for 90 seconds.

5 Pour the spice mixture into the lentils and stir thoroughly to combine. Serve garnished with fresh coriander sprigs.

CHEF'S TIPS:
   Place the mug on a small plate whilst
      cooking in the microwave to catch
         any overflows.
         If you don't have all the spices, use
      ready-made curry powder.

This recipe is inspired by a meal I had in a beautiful little town called Hangzhou in the Zhejiang Province of Eastern China. It is a dark and sultry dish; the aubergines are cooked until soft and succulent, soaking up all the instense flavours of the garlic, chilli, ginger and soy.

FIERY AUBERGINE WITH PORK IN SOY

SERVES 1
COOKING TIME: 6 minutes
   (800W microwave)
EQUIPMENT: 500ml/17fl oz
   mug

1 clove garlic, finely chopped
15ml/1 tbsp fresh root ginger,
   grated
30ml/2 tbsp chopped fresh
   red chilli, plus extra
   to garnish

15ml/1 tbsp soy sauce
15ml/1 tbsp rice wine vinegar
7.5ml/1½ tsp clear honey
150g/5oz aubergine/
   eggplant, diced
50g/2oz minced/ground pork
7.5ml/1½ tsp sesame oil
1 spring onion/scallion, sliced
Salt and ground black
   pepper
Pinch sesame seeds
   (optional)

1 Add the garlic, ginger, chilli, soy sauce, rice wine vinegar and honey to the mug and combine well.

2 Add the aubergine and gently fold in, then add the pork in small clumps. Cover the mug and microwave on full power for 4 minutes.

3 Remove the cover, break up the pork clumps and stir gently. Add the sesame oil, season and microwave uncovered for a further 2 minutes.

4 Mix through the spring onions and garnish with extra sliced chilli and sesame seeds, if using.

CHEF'S TIPS:
You can substitute regular malt vinegar for the rice wine vinegar.
   To create a vegetarian version you can substitute green beans for the pork.

This is a total guilty pleasure of mine – I always end up ordering this in our local Italian restaurant. Spaghetti carbonara is a wonderfully classic recipe that when done right is a real thing of beauty, letting the eggs create a deliciously creamy and authentic sauce.

SURPRISINGLY AUTHENTIC SPAGHETTI CARBONARA

SERVES 1
COOKING TIME: 9 minutes
(800W microwave)
EQUIPMENT: 500ml/17fl oz
mug, bowl

60g/2¼oz smoked pancetta,
  finely diced
½ clove garlic, left whole
80g/3¼oz dried spaghetti,
  broken in half

300ml/½ pint/1¼ cups water,
  just boiled
15g/½oz Parmesan cheese,
  grated
1 egg yolk
15ml/1 tbsp chopped fresh
  parsley
Ground black pepper

1 Microwave the pancetta and garlic on full power for 2 minutes uncovered in a mug. Remove from the microwave, pour away the excess oil, discard the garlic and set the mug aside whilst you make the pasta.

2 Place the dried pasta and just-boiled water in a bowl and cook on full power uncovered for 7 minutes.

3 Add the Parmesan cheese, egg yolk and ground black pepper to the cooked pancetta in the mug and mix thoroughly.

4 Once the pasta is done, the cooking water will be very hot; remove from the microwave carefully, and slowly add 15ml/1 tbsp of the cooking water to the carbonara paste in the mug and combine.

5 Using a slotted spoon add the pasta to the paste and stir through (you want the pasta to still be a bit wet to help thicken the sauce). Serve immediately garnished with a sprinkle of freshly chopped parsley.

CHEF'S TIPS:
I've developed this recipe specifically to be executed in the order above which ensures everything gets combined at the right temperatures to create a creamy sauce and not scrambled eggs!
  If you can't find pancetta you can always use smoked streaky/fatty bacon instead.
  I've not included any salt as the pancetta and Parmesan cheese are usually enough but taste to ensure it pleases your palate.
  If you do want this to be extra creamy you could add a teaspoon of double/heavy cream at the end, but it won't be Surprisingly Authentic!

This is one of those dishes that you won't actually believe you've created so quickly or easily. Everything gets prepared in advance and then you just pop it in the microwave for six minutes and you're done! I like to slice my chicken breast before serving just to make it look a little bit fancy…

STUFFED CHICKEN BREAST WITH CHICKPEAS

SERVES **1**

COOKING TIME: **6 minutes (800W microwave), plus 2 minutes standing**

EQUIPMENT: **500ml/17fl oz mug**

Pinch chilli flakes

50g/2oz canned chickpeas, drained and rinsed

90ml/3fl oz canned chopped tomatoes

15ml/1 tbsp olive oil

100–130g/3¾–4½oz chicken breast, skinned

30ml/2 tbsp cream cheese

20g/¾oz black olives, pitted and diced

30g/1¼oz pancetta rashers/strips

5ml/1 tsp chopped fresh parsley

Salt and ground black pepper

1 Mix the chilli flakes, chickpeas, tomatoes and olive oil in the mug.

2 Prepare the chicken breast: using a sharp pointed knife cut into the side of the chicken breast to create a pocket; try not to pierce the other side. Stuff the chicken breast with as much of the cream cheese as possible and three-quarters of the olives, but leave enough room to just close the pocket.

3 Lay the pancetta rashers on a chopping board, slightly overlapping to create a 'sheet' of pancetta.

4 Lay the stuffed chicken breast on top of the pancetta with the incision going across the pancetta rashers. Wrap the pancetta around the chicken breast and trim any ends of the chicken that stick out (but be careful not to cut into the pocket)!

5 Rest the wrapped chicken breast on top of the chickpea and tomato mixture in the mug and microwave uncovered on full power for 6 minutes. Leave to stand for 2 minutes before garnishing with parsley, seasoning and eating.

CHEF'S TIPS:

This is pretty much foolproof, but try to use a small chicken breast approximately 100g/3¾oz in weight; if you do have a much larger chicken breast trim if possible, or alternatively increase the cooking time.

To really show off this recipe, pour the sauce on to a serving plate, slice the chicken breast in three across the width and lay on top of the chickpea sauce.

You may find it easier to mix the cream cheese and olives together before stuffing into the chicken pocket.

Transport your tastebuds to a Spanish island with a delicious combination of flavours: heady chorizo, earthy goat's cheese, creamy avocado… This is one of those dishes that is both perfect for a summertime lunch or a winter comfort blanket. Simply cooked but complex in taste, it is one to enjoy.

CHORIZO, LENTIL AND GOAT'S CHEESE

SERVES 1
COOKING TIME: **1 minute**
   (800W microwave)
EQUIPMENT: **300ml/½ pint**
   mug

25g/1oz red bell pepper, thinly sliced
40g/1½oz baby plum tomatoes, sliced
15ml/1 tbsp extra virgin olive oil, plus extra for drizzling
70g/2¾oz pre-cooked puy lentils

30g/1¼oz chorizo, sliced
2.5ml/½ tsp water
30ml/2 tbsp chopped fresh parsley
7.5ml/1½ tsp lemon juice
50g/2oz/about ½ a small avocado, cut into chunks
30g/1¼oz goat's cheese, ripped into small pieces
Salt and ground black pepper

1 Add the red pepper, tomatoes, olive oil, lentils, chorizo and water to the mug and microwave covered on full power for 1 minute.

2 Add the parsley and lemon juice, season heavily and combine. Then gently fold in the avocado and the goat's cheese.

3 Serve with an extra drizzle of olive oil, if required.

CHEF'S TIPS:
To stop the avocado from turning brown, rub some lemon juice over the flesh.
   Remember to check if you need to peel the skin off the chorizo as some types sold in shops do not have edible skins.

A good friend of mine from Mexico introduced me to the flavours of chipotle chillies and I've been addicted ever since. The delicious combination of heat, smoke and sweetness unique to chipotles is now available in supermarkets as a paste. This particular dish marries chipotle with classic Mexican corn.

MEXICAN CHICKEN AND CHIPOTLE

SERVES **1**

COOKING TIME: **5 minutes (800W microwave), plus 3 minutes standing**

EQUIPMENT: **300ml/½ pint mug**

80g/3¼oz corn kernels
100g/3¾oz chicken breast, thinly sliced (about the thickness of a coin)
1 clove garlic, grated
1 spring onion/scallion, finely sliced
30g/1¼oz tomatoes, roughly diced
30ml/2 tbsp olive oil
5ml/1 tsp vinegar
2.5ml/½ tsp dried oregano
2.5ml/½ tsp smoked paprika
15ml/1 tbsp chipotle paste
22.5ml/1½ tbsp water
Few sprigs fresh coriander/ cilantro

1 Add all the ingredients, except the coriander, to the mug. Cover and microwave on full power for 3 minutes.

2 Remove from the microwave, stir and then microwave on full power again for a further 2 minutes uncovered. Remove from the microwave, stir and leave to stand for 3 minutes

3 Garnish with fresh coriander leaves.

CHEF'S TIPS:
You can buy chipotle paste from most supermarkets – check the heat as some are hotter than others so you may want to decrease or increase the quantity at your discretion!
   You can also garnish with fresh chopped chilli for an extra fiery kick.
   If you don't have fresh, frozen corn is fine.

There is something about lemons and summer that just seem to complement each other so well. But this recipe is great all year round – a warm salad that is filling, tasty and healthy. You can find orzo in most supermarkets and it is a very versatile ingredient to have in your store cupboard.

WARM ORZO AND LEMON CHICKEN

SERVES 1
COOKING TIME: 7 minutes
   (800W microwave), plus
   1 minute standing
EQUIPMENT: 300ml/½ pint
   mug

30g/1¼oz orzo
150ml/5fl oz/⅔ cup hot water
80g/3¼oz chicken breast,
   sliced into bitesize pieces
1 clove garlic, sliced
50g/2oz courgette/
   zucchini, diced
30ml/2 tbsp cold water

30g/1¼oz/3 cherry tomatoes,
   finely diced
Juice and zest ¼ lemon
15ml/1 tbsp extra virgin
   olive oil
15ml/1 tbsp chopped fresh
   coriander/cilantro
15ml/1 tbsp chopped fresh
   parsley
Salt and ground black
   pepper

1 Place the orzo and hot water in the mug and microwave uncovered on full power for 5 minutes. (Put the mug on a plate to catch any overflow of water.)

2 Add the chicken, garlic, courgette and cold water and gently push the ingredients down into the mug with a fork. Microwave covered on full power for 2 minutes. Leave to stand for 1 minute before removing the cover.

3 Add the tomatoes, lemon juice and zest, olive oil, fresh coriander and parsley and stir gently to combine. Season to taste.

CHEF'S TIP:
Add a few leaves of spinach or kale at the end for some extra greens!

An authentic biryani is a work of art and a labour of love. My super-quick version has been developed to give the same satisfaction but in a fraction of the time. Heady aromatics of India entwined with perfectly cooked rice and laced with succulent chicken make this a dish to set your tastebuds alight.

QUICK CHICKEN BIRYANI

SERVES 1
COOKING TIME: 10 minutes (800W microwave), plus 5 minutes standing
EQUIPMENT: 300ml/½ pint mug

35g/1⅓oz onion, finely sliced
1 large clove garlic, diced
2.5cm/½in piece fresh root ginger, grated
30ml/2 tbsp rapeseed or vegetable oil
7.5ml/1½ tsp butter
1.5ml/¼ tsp salt
Pinch ground black pepper
2.5ml/½ tsp turmeric
2.5ml/½ tsp ground cumin
2.5ml/½ tsp garam masala
2.5ml/½ tsp chilli powder

2.5ml/½ tsp ground cinnamon
40g/1½oz basmati rice, rinsed
3 green cardamom pods
3 cloves
1 stick cinnamon, about 2.5cm/1in long
6 threads saffron, soaked in 60ml/2fl oz/¼ cup water or chicken stock
100g/3¾oz chicken breast, cut into bitesize pieces
1.5ml/¼ tsp sugar
120ml/4fl oz/½ cup hot water or chicken stock
10g/¼oz flaked/sliced almonds
10g/¼oz raisins or sultanas/ golden raisins
Few fresh coriander/ cilantro leaves

1 Add the onion, garlic, ginger, oil, butter, seasoning and all the ground spices to the mug and microwave uncovered on full power for 3 minutes. Remove from the microwave and stir well.

2 Add the rice, whole spices, saffron with its soaking liquid, chicken pieces and sugar to the ground spice mixture in the mug and combine thoroughly. Microwave uncovered on full power for 2 minutes and then stir well once again.

3 Add 30ml/1fl oz/⅛ cup of the hot water or stock to the mug, stir and microwave uncovered for 3 minutes.

4 Add another 45ml/1.5fl oz of water or stock, cover the mug and microwave on full power for 2 minutes.

5 Stir in the remaining 45ml/1.5fl oz water or stock, flaked almonds, raisins or sultanas and the fresh coriander, re-cover and leave to stand for 5 minutes.

CHEF'S TIP:
You could swap all the ground spices for a pre-made curry powder if you haven't got them all in your store cupboard.

This is a really nice alternative to the usual risotto, with a Greek twist. The halloumi just melts in your mouth but keeps its texture, combined with a layer of citrus from the lemon juice. You'll notice that unlike most risottos this recipe doesn't use any butter, making it a very light, summery dish.

HELLENIC CHICKEN AND LEMON RISOTTO

SERVES 1
COOKING TIME: 11½ minutes (800W microwave), plus 5 minutes standing
EQUIPMENT: 500ml/17fl oz mug

15g/½oz onion, finely diced
1 clove garlic, sliced
15ml/1 tbsp olive oil, plus extra for drizzling
50g/2oz Arborio rice
90g/3½oz chicken breast, chopped and skinned (save the skin – see Chef's Tip!)

250ml/8fl oz/1 cup chicken stock or water
40g/1½oz frozen peas
30g/1¼oz halloumi cheese, diced
30ml/2 tbsp chopped fresh mint leaves
15ml/1 tbsp lemon juice
Few grates lemon zest
Salt and ground black pepper

1 Add the onion, garlic, olive oil and seasoning to the mug and microwave uncovered on full power for 90 seconds.

2 Add the rice, chicken and 125ml/4fl oz/½ cup of the stock, stir in and then microwave covered for 3 minutes.

3 Remove from the microwave, stir, re-cover and microwave again for 3 minutes without adding any more liquid.

4 Remove from the microwave, add 75ml/2.5fl oz/⅓ cup stock and the frozen peas and microwave covered for 3 minutes.

5 Add the remaining 50ml/2fl oz/¼ cup stock and the halloumi and microwave uncovered for a final 1 minute. Stir in the fresh mint and lemon juice and leave to stand for 5 minutes.

6 Garnish with a drizzle of olive oil and few grates of lemon zest. Taste for seasoning; depending on the saltiness of the halloumi you may not need to add any more salt but be sure to add a good hit of black pepper!

CHEF'S TIP:
If you want to really increase the level of chicken flavour, place the chicken skin on a plate, season with a little salt and microwave for 2 minutes uncovered. It will sound like a war-zone in your microwave but you'll be rewarded with some delicious chicken-skin crackling! Yes, that's right, chicken-skin crackling. Leave it for a minute to relax and it will crisp up beautifully. Chop this up as a garnish or stir through the risotto.

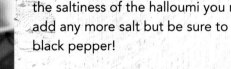

FAST FISH (& SPEEDY SEAFOOD)

Microwaves almost seem as if they were invented to cook fish and seafood. If the fish or seafood is within a sauce it doesn't usually take very long for the fish to be cooked in the heat of the surrounding liquid. But where the microwave really shows off its affinity to cook fish is when it is steamed. The secret is for the fish to have some liquid in the mug that the microwave can turn to steam. So a dash of water, or the natural moisture in a tomato, keeps the fish succulent, moist and perfectly cooked.

This dish is the epitome of a Mediterranean summer. Clean, delicate flakes of perfectly cooked cod resting on a rich tomato and aubergine base with a hint of garlic. This is one of those recipes that demonstrates the benefits of microwave cooking by creating an entire meal in a matter of minutes – and it is also healthy!

MEDITERRANEAN COD ON AUBERGINE

SERVES 1
COOKING TIME: 2–3 minutes (800W microwave)
EQUIPMENT: 500ml/17fl oz mug

1 slice of aubergine/ eggplant, approx. 50g/ 2oz, cut widthways 5cm/2in thick
1 clove garlic, cut in half lengthways
15ml/1 tbsp extra virgin olive oil, plus extra for drizzling
25g/1oz baby plum tomatoes, roughly chopped
6 fresh basil leaves, torn, plus a few extra to garnish
2.5ml/½ tsp balsamic vinegar
90g/3½oz cod steak, skinned
Salt and ground black pepper

1 Wipe the cut side of the garlic clove over both sides of the aubergine slice and then wipe olive oil on to both sides. Place the prepared aubergine in the bottom of the mug; you may need to cut the slice into quarters to fit.

2 Place the tomatoes on top of the aubergine, reserving a few tomatoes, then add the torn basil leaves, drizzle with balsamic vinegar and finally put the cod steak on top.

3 Place the remaining plum tomatoes on top of the cod, drizzle with olive oil and loosely cover with clear film or plastic wrap, ensuring that the edges are sealed around the mug and piercing the clear film several times.

4 Microwave on full power for 3 minutes; if the cod steak is quite flat 2 minutes should be enough.

5 Remove the cover and serve garnished with a few basil leaves and seasoned with salt and pepper.

CHEF'S TIP:
A pinch of dried chilli flakes adds a tasty extra garnish. And a piece of fresh bread is great to mop up all those lovely juices!

The potatoes make this a wonderfully creamy and thick chowder without having to add any cream, so it is a filling but not a heavy meal. I also really enjoy having little pockets of crunchy sweetness from the corn in an otherwise earthy smoky dish.

SMOKED HADDOCK CHOWDER

SERVES 1
COOKING TIME: 7 minutes (800W microwave), plus 1 minute standing
EQUIPMENT: 300ml/½ pint mug

80g/3¼oz peeled potatoes, diced into small cubes
15ml/1 tbsp butter
1 bay leaf
30ml/2 tbsp water
45ml/3 tbsp milk
30g/1¼oz frozen corn kernels
2.5ml/½ tsp English mustard
80g/3¼oz skinned smoked haddock, cut into cubes
15ml/1 tbsp chopped fresh parsley
Salt and ground black pepper

1 Add the potatoes, butter, bay leaf and water to the mug, cover and microwave on full power for 5 minutes.

2 Remove the bay leaf and mash the potatoes with a fork until they are as smooth as possible.

3 Add a third of the milk and whisk together to form a paste, then add the remaining milk, corn, mustard, seasoning and stir thoroughly to combine.

4 Fold in the smoked haddock, replace the bay leaf and microwave covered on full power for a further 2 minutes, then leave to stand for a minute.

5 Remove the bay leaf, stir gently, and garnish with chopped fresh parsley.

CHEF'S TIPS:
Experiment with other vegetables – peas work very well, as does a tiny pinch of cayenne pepper for garnish and warmth.

If you're happy to forgo the healthy option, add another small knob of butter at the same time as the fish or a small drizzle of cream with the parsley for an extra indulgent chowder.

I don't know anyone that doesn't enjoy a good paella, and if I did I would have to disown them as a friend! This paella recipe infuses the Arborio rice with the heady fragrance of saffron and smoky paprika and brings a little Spanish sunshine to your dining table.

SEAFOOD PAELLA

SERVES 1
COOKING TIME: 13–16
minutes (800W
microwave), plus
5 minutes standing
EQUIPMENT: bowl, 500ml/
17fl oz mug

8 saffron threads
275–325ml/9½–11fl oz/
generous 1–1⅓ cups
chicken stock
20g/¾oz onion, grated
1 clove garlic, grated
5ml/1 tsp smoked paprika

5ml/1 tsp tomato
purée/paste
15ml/1 tbsp olive oil, plus
extra for drizzling
20g/¾oz green bell
pepper, diced
50g/2oz Arborio rice
6 king prawns/jumbo shrimp
2 baby squid, cut into rings
about finger width
Few fresh coriander/cilantro
sprigs, to garnish
Squeeze lemon juice
Salt and ground black
pepper

1 Place the saffron threads in 125ml/4fl oz/generous ½ cup of the chicken stock in a bowl and set aside to soak.

2 Place the onion, garlic, paprika, tomato purée, olive oil, green pepper and seasoning in the mug and microwave uncovered on full power for 2 minutes.

3 Add the rice and saffron with its soaking stock, and combine thoroughly. Microwave for 3 minutes covered on full power, remove from the microwave and stir well.

4 Add 50ml/2fl oz/¼ cup of stock and microwave for 3 minutes uncovered on full power.

5 Add a further 50ml/2fl oz/¼ cup of stock and microwave again for 3 minutes – the rice should feel just cooked, a little al dente, if it is not repeat the process of adding stock and cooking for 3 minutes.

6 Finally add the prawns, squid and a final 50ml/2fl oz/¼ cup stock and microwave for 2 minutes.

7 Stir, leave to stand for 5 minutes, and season to taste. Serve garnished with fresh coriander, a squeeze of lemon juice and a little drizzle of olive oil.

CHEF'S TIP:
If you can't find saffron use a paella seasoning mix. Keep tasting the rice through the cycles until it is almost done then add the seafood for the final cooking process. The rice and seafood will continue to cook whilst standing. Add more stock after standing if too thick.

This recipe started life as an experiment a few years ago when I just wanted a bit more bang for my buck in terms of flavour when I was making a fish pie. This is my microwaved version with a subtle hint of Indian spice, giving a little twist on tradition and an added warmth of flavour.

CURRIED FISH PIE

SERVES 1
**COOKING TIME: 7 minutes
(800W microwave), plus
1 minute standing**
**EQUIPMENT: 300ml/½ pint
mug**

60g/2¼oz potato, diced
15ml/1 tbsp butter
15ml/1 tbsp flour
90ml/3fl oz/generous ⅓ cup
milk
80g/3¼oz frozen peas
100g/3¾oz mixed fish, eg
salmon, smoked haddock,
cod, etc, cubed

3 king prawns/jumbo shrimp,
cut in half
½ clove garlic, grated
1cm/½in piece fresh root
ginger, grated
5ml/1 tsp curry powder, plus
extra for sprinkling, see
Chef's Tip
Few sprigs fresh parsley or
coriander/cilantro,
to garnish
Salt and ground black
pepper

1 Mix the diced potato with the butter in the mug, cover and microwave on full power for 3 minutes.

2 Add the flour to the potatoes and butter and mix to form a lumpy paste (you will have lumps of potato in the paste – it doesn't matter).

3 Very slowly add the milk – add just a few drops, mix, then a few more drops until you have a smooth paste with the lumps of potato. Add all the remaining ingredients, apart from the garnish, combine well, cover and microwave for 2 minutes.

4 Stir and leave to stand for a minute. Cover and microwave again for a further 2 minutes.

5 Gently stir, being careful not to break up all the fish. Serve garnished with the parsley or coriander, a sprinkling of curry powder and seasoned to taste.

CHEF'S TIP:
If you prefer to make your own curry powder, combine a pinch each of turmeric, cumin, garam masala, ground chilli powder and ground cinnamon.

This dish is like healthy junk food; totally satisfying to eat yet packed with fresh, nutritious ingredients. Seabass is used a lot in Asian cooking and I find the meaty texture and taste holds up well against strong flavours, complementing the seasoned noodles really well.

STEAMED GINGER SEABASS ON NOODLES

SERVES 1
COOKING TIME: 6½ minutes
(800W microwave), plus
2 minutes standing
EQUIPMENT: 500ml/17fl oz
mug

50g/2oz dried egg noodles,
broken
50g/2oz pak choi/bok choy,
roughly chopped
1 button/white mushroom,
sliced

1 clove garlic, sliced
½ red chilli, chopped, plus
extra to garnish
5ml/1 tsp light soy sauce
2.5ml/½ tsp honey or soft
light brown sugar
7.5ml/1½ tsp sesame oil
70g/2¾oz/½ seabass fillet
2.5cm/1in piece fresh root
ginger, grated

1 Place the broken noodles in the mug and cover with boiling water. Microwave on full power uncovered for 4½ minutes.

2 Drain the water from the noodles and add the pak choi, mushroom, garlic, chilli, soy sauce, honey or sugar and half the sesame oil and combine well with the noodles.

3 Then place the seabass on top of the noodles and scatter the ginger on top of the seabass. Drizzle the remaining sesame oil over the top, cover and microwave for 2 minutes on full power, then leave to stand for 2 minutes. Serve garnished with some extra chilli.

CHEF'S TIPS:
There is no need to peel the fresh root ginger, just grate it with the skin on.
 You can also try this dish with haddock or salmon.

Travelling throughout Asia you notice certain ingredients are ubiquitous, such as coconut, chilli, lemon grass and fish sauce. For good reason: put these humble ingredients together and they create magic. Inspired by the popular Tom Kha soup, this is my seafood version of a Thai classic.

ASIAN COCONUT SOUP

SERVES 1
COOKING TIME: 3½ minutes (800W microwave), plus 2 minutes standing
EQUIPMENT: 500ml/ 17fl oz mug

100g/3¾oz mixed frozen shellfish
½ pak choi/bok choy, cut into thirds lengthways
2 spring onions/scallions, finely sliced
1 red chilli, sliced
2.5cm/1in piece fresh root ginger, cut into thin julienne strips

½ clove garlic, finely sliced
1 stick of lemon grass, bottom half finely sliced, top half reserved
2.5ml/½ tsp sesame oil
5ml/1 tsp vegetable oil
45ml/3 tbsp water
125ml/4fl oz/generous ½ cup coconut milk
15ml/1 tbsp fish sauce
Juice ¼ lime
15ml/1 tbsp chopped fresh coriander/cilantro
3 button/white mushrooms, thinly sliced

1 Place the shellfish, pak choi, spring onions, chilli, ginger, garlic, sliced lemon grass, oils and water together in the mug and microwave covered on full power for 2 minutes.

2 Remove from the microwave and add all the remaining ingredients, including the top half of the lemon grass, and microwave uncovered on full power for 90 seconds.

3 Leave to stand for 2 minutes before removing the stick of lemon grass, and it is ready to serve.

CHEF'S TIPS:
When cutting the lemon grass, peel the first couple of layers away and cut the stalk just above the root end.
 This is a really versatile soup which works equally well if you exchange the shellfish for cubed white fish (such as sustainable cod or haddock) or chicken, or make a vegetarian version using broccoli, cauliflower and peas.

This really gets the tastebuds going, with lots of Asian flavour, and makes a great quick lunch that isn't too heavy. I like it hot and the dried chilli flakes give a smokier flavour than using fresh chillies which would give it a fruity heat. Feel free to tone it down by reducing or omitting the chilli.

CHILLI SALMON AND SPINACH SALAD

SERVES 1
COOKING TIME: 2½ minutes
   (800W microwave)
EQUIPMENT: 500ml/17fl oz
   mug

100g/3¾oz salmon, cubed
30ml/2 tbsp olive oil
7.5ml/1½ tsp sesame oil
2.5cm/1in piece fresh root
   ginger, grated

1 clove garlic, grated
2.5ml/½ tsp dried chilli flakes
7.5ml/1½ tsp light soy sauce
Pinch sugar
Salt and ground black
   pepper
20g/¾oz baby leaf spinach,
   roughly sliced
Few fresh coriander/cilantro
   leaves, gently ripped

1 Add all the ingredients, except the spinach and coriander, to the mug and microwave covered on full power for 1½ minutes.

2 Remove from the microwave, stir and microwave covered for a further minute.

3 Remove the cover and immediately (but gently!) stir through the spinach and coriander.

CHEF'S TIPS:
You can make this dish as hot or not as you want by changing the amount of dried chilli flakes used.

Really good quality chilli flakes in oil (found in most Chinese supermarkets) are a great addition for some oriental heat.

You can add other vegetable ingredients with the raw spinach, such as pak choi/bok choy, beansprouts, thinly sliced carrot or even cucumber.

If you wanted to make this a more substantial meal add some cooked noodles.

This is definitely a personal favourite. Based on a traditional village-style recipe this seafood pasta will take your tastebuds on a journey to the Mediterranean. But be warned – there is plenty of garlic in this so be sure to share it with your loved one; otherwise you can forget about any stolen kisses!

STOLEN KISS SEAFOOD PASTA

SERVES 1
COOKING TIME: 12½ minutes
(800W microwave), plus
2 minutes standing
EQUIPMENT: 500ml/17fl oz
mug, bowl

80g/3¼oz dried spaghetti, broken in half
300ml/10fl oz/1¼ cups hot water
1 clove garlic, sliced
45ml/3 tbsp extra virgin olive oil
8 baby plum tomatoes or 60g/2¼oz ripe tomatoes, cut into halves
100g/3¾oz mixed frozen shellfish
30ml/2 tbsp chopped fresh parsley
Pinch dried chilli flakes

1 Place the spaghetti and the hot water into a bowl and microwave uncovered on full power for 7 minutes. Set aside with the pasta resting in the water.

2 Place the garlic, olive oil and tomatoes in the mug and microwave uncovered on full power for 3 minutes.

3 Add the shellfish and microwave uncovered for a further 2 minutes.

4 Drain the pasta and add to the shellfish mixture in the mug with 15ml/1 tbsp of the cooking water, and microwave uncovered for 30 seconds, to help the pasta absorb all those lovely flavours.

5 Garnish with the parsley and chilli flakes and leave to stand for 2 minutes.

CHEF'S TIPS:
If you want to jazz this up a little you can add a tablespoon of Ouzo or white wine at stage 2. But I figure if you open a bottle of wine for 1 tablespoon in this recipe it would be rude not to enjoy a glass with your meal as well!
    You can usually find packets of frozen shellfish mixes in your local supermarket.

There is something seductively alluring about this dark, sultry risotto. A little squid ink goes a long way and gives this risotto a very subtle taste of the ocean. Surprisingly this was also one of the favourites for the Recipe Development Tasting Team (also known as my children).

SQUID INK RISOTTO

SERVES 1
COOKING TIME: 10 minutes (800W microwave), plus 2 minutes standing
EQUIPMENT: 500ml/17fl oz mug

20g/¾oz onion, diced
1 clove garlic, finely diced
30ml/2 tbsp olive oil
60g/2¼oz Arborio rice
2.5ml/½ tsp/1 sachet squid ink

455ml/15½fl oz/scant 2 cups fish stock
60g/2¼oz squid, cut into 5cm/2in squares
7.5ml/1½ tsp butter
15ml/1 tbsp chopped fresh parsley, plus extra to garnish
¼ fresh red chilli, thinly sliced
7.5ml/1½ tsp lemon juice
Salt and ground black pepper

CHEF'S TIPS:
If you want to increase the wow factor you can cook the tentacles for 45 seconds separately and place them on top of the mug to give you a striking contrast of white squid and black risotto.

If you don't have fish stock or bouillon cubes, you could reserve a little of the squid ink to stir through at the end to increase the ocean flavour of the dish. Equally you could cheat by adding 2.5ml/½ tsp of Thai fish sauce.

1 Combine the onion, garlic and half the olive oil together in the mug and microwave uncovered on full power for 2 minutes.

2 Add the rice and squid ink and stir thoroughly to coat the rice. Add 100ml/3.5fl oz/scant ½ cup of the stock and microwave uncovered for 2 minutes.

3 Add the squid and 75ml/2.5fl oz/⅓ cup of the stock and microwave uncovered for 3 minutes.

4 Add another 75ml/2.5fl oz/⅓ cup stock and microwave uncovered for 3 minutes until the stock has been absorbed. Repeat the process with the remaining stock until the rice is cooked to your preference.

5 Finally stir through the butter and chopped parsley. Garnish with the chilli, lemon juice, a little extra parsley and the remaining olive oil. Leave to stand for 2 minutes. Season to taste and serve.

A simple yet stunning summer dish, full of delicious ingredients that feels like lunch in Provence. This recipe really brings out the flavours of the tomatoes, complementing the courgettes and lemon. Steaming the salmon keeps it very moist and succulent whilst cooking it to perfection!

PROVENÇAL PEAS & SALMON

SERVES **1**
COOKING TIME: **3 minutes**
  (**800W microwave**)
EQUIPMENT: **500ml/17fl oz**
  mug

120ml/4fl oz/½ cup canned
  marrowfat peas (keep some
  of the juice from the can)
30g/1¼oz/¼ courgette/
  zucchini, diced
60g/2¼oz/4 cherry tomatoes,
  cut into halves

¼ clove garlic, grated
15ml/1 tbsp chopped
  fresh parsley
45ml/3 tbsp extra virgin
  olive oil
90g/3½oz salmon fillet
15ml/1 tbsp lemon juice
½ jalapeño chilli, chopped
  (optional)
Salt and ground black
  pepper

1 Combine the peas and some of the juice with the courgette, tomatoes, garlic, parsley and 30ml/2 tbsp of the olive oil in the mug, and season.

2 Cut the salmon fillet in half, place on top of the vegetable mixture and spoon a little of the mixture over the fish. Microwave covered on full power for 3 minutes.

3 Remove from the microwave and drizzle over the remaining 15ml/1 tbsp olive oil, the lemon juice and the chilli, if using.

CHEF'S TIPS:
The marrowfat peas work perfectly with some of their juice to create a sauce for this dish, but you can experiment by adding different vegetables or even beans for a heartier meal.
   This dish goes well served with some fresh bread to mop up the juices.

My Dad (aka 'Paps') kindly donated (I stole) this recipe and it is a big favourite of the kids. This is a simple dish that works really well in the microwave; the juices from the mussels combine with the butter and garlic to create a deliciously rich sauce which the children devour, enjoying anything that allows them to get messy.

PAPS MAGIC MUSSELS

SERVES 1
COOKING TIME: 2 minutes
 (800W microwave)
EQUIPMENT: 500ml/17fl oz
 mug

300g/11oz live mussels,
 scrubbed
7.5ml/1½ tsp water

1 clove garlic, finely chopped
15ml/1 tbsp butter
15ml/1 tbsp olive oil
2.5ml/½ tsp chopped fresh
 red chilli
2.5ml/½ tsp lemon juice
15ml/1 tbsp chopped fresh
 parsley

1 Add the mussels to the mug first, then the water, garlic, butter, olive oil and chilli. Cover with clear film or plastic wrap (don't pierce) and microwave on full power for 2 minutes.

2 Remove the covering, being careful of the hot steam. Drizzle over the lemon juice and a scattering of parsley. Gently fold the mussels into the sauce. Sit down and enjoy!

CHEF'S TIPS:
Make sure you use clear film or plastic wrap to cover the mussels as they will expand when they open, stretching the film. If you use a plate it may well topple off.
   The general rule with mussels is to check that they are closed before cooking (this shows they are still alive) and only eat the ones that open once cooked. However any closed mussels after cooking should be discarded.

VEGETABLES & VEGETARIAN

Contrary to popular belief vegetables are one of the ingredients that take the longest to cook in the microwave besides pasta and rice. All the root vegetables (carrots, potatoes, etc.) are very dense and so the microwave has to work hard in shaking all those molecules to cook them. However the softer vegetables – green beans, asparagus, tomatoes – do cook much more quickly. Here are some delicious and hearty vegetable and vegetarian recipes that make a great meal for anyone.

There are a few secrets in cooking and with a risotto it is all about the stock. The better the stock the better the risotto. My mushroom risotto uses dried porcini mushrooms to create a strong stock that soaks into the rice to give a real funghi hit! Plus the added secret ingredient of almond liqueur.

DECADENT MUSHROOM RISOTTO WITH PINE NUTS

SERVES 1
COOKING TIME: 10–14
 minutes (800W
 microwave), plus 10
 minutes soaking and
 2 minutes standing
EQUIPMENT: 500ml/17fl oz
 mug, bowl

10g/¼oz dried mushrooms
 (porcini or mixed is fine)
300ml/10fl oz/1¼ cups water,
 just boiled
15g/½oz onion, diced
1 clove garlic, chopped
2 button/white mushrooms,
 sliced

15ml/1 tbsp olive oil, plus
 extra for drizzling
5ml/1 tsp almond liqueur,
 such as Disaronno
 or a brandy
50g/2oz Arborio rice
7.5ml/1½ tsp butter
30ml/2 tbsp chopped fresh
 parsley
15ml/1 tbsp grated Parmesan
 cheese
7.5ml/1½ tsp pine nuts,
 toasted
Salt and ground black
 pepper

1 Soak the dried mushrooms in the water for 10 minutes in a bowl. Drain the mushrooms, reserving the stock and squeezing out the excess liquid. Then finely chop the mushrooms.

2 Place the onion, garlic, button mushrooms and olive oil in the mug and microwave uncovered on full power for 2 minutes.

3 Then add the almond liqueur or brandy, rice and 120ml/4fl oz/½ cup of the mushroom stock and microwave covered for 3 minutes. Remove the cover, stir and then microwave uncovered for another 3 minutes.

4 Add 60ml/2fl oz/¼ cup more stock and microwave covered on full power for 2 minutes – repeat this process until all the stock is used or the rice is cooked al dente, you don't want it mushy.

5 Add the soaked chopped mushrooms, butter, parsley and Parmesan and stir well. Leave to stand for 2 minutes and then garnish with the pine nuts and a drizzle of olive oil. Season to taste.

CHEF'S TIP:
Try adding chopped sage to the risotto for an earthier taste – but use sparingly as it is a strong flavour!

A clean wholesome meal that is delicate in flavour yet hearty, and with a vibrant citrus note. There is something very pure and honest about a humble white bean stew. This village food recipe works perfectly as a dish in its own right but also makes an excellent accompaniment in a larger meal.

WHITE BEAN AND CITRUS CASSOULET

SERVES 1
COOKING TIME: 7 minutes
   (800W microwave)
EQUIPMENT: 500ml/17fl oz
   mug

30ml/2 tbsp olive oil
20g/¾oz/about ¼ medium
   carrot, finely sliced
15g/½oz onion, diced
1 clove garlic, diced
3 button/white mushrooms,
   sliced
30g/1¼oz potato, diced

20g/¾oz/about 2 cherry
   tomatoes, chopped
Pinch salt
100g/3¾oz canned cannellini
   beans, drained and rinsed
30g/1¼oz Little Gem/Bibb
   lettuce, cut into 2.5cm/
   1in strips
75ml/2½fl oz/⅓ cup water
15ml/1 tbsp lemon juice
15ml/1 tbsp chopped fresh
   parsley
Salt and ground black
   pepper

1 Place half the olive oil, the carrot, onion, garlic, mushrooms, potato, tomatoes and salt together in the mug and microwave covered on full power for 4 minutes.

2 Then add the cannellini beans, lettuce and water to the mug and microwave uncovered on full power for 3 minutes.

3 Finally stir through the lemon juice, the remaining olive oil and parsley, and season to taste.

CHEF'S TIP:
If you can, try to buy as good quality cannellini beans as possible as these really are the star of the show. Butter/lima beans would also work well in this recipe.

Whilst travelling through India I stayed in Udaipur where the famous palace
on a lake resides. It was here that I was lucky enough to be invited to cook
with a local lady and her daughter who taught me some of their traditional
homemade dishes. This recipe is inspired by that afternoon in their home.

BOMBAY CAULIFLOWER

SERVES 1
**COOKING TIME: 6 minutes
(800W microwave), plus
1 minute standing**
**EQUIPMENT: 300ml/½ pint
mug**

60g/2¼oz cauliflower, cut into
small florets
20g/¾oz onion, finely diced
1 clove garlic, diced
7.5ml/1½ tsp grated fresh
root ginger
15ml/1 tbsp
vegetable oil
7.5ml/1½ tsp butter

30g/1¼oz frozen peas
40g/1½oz canned chickpeas,
drained and rinsed
60ml/4 tbsp canned
tomatoes
2.5ml/½ tsp tumeric
2.5ml/½ tsp ground cumin
2.5ml/½ tsp garam masala
2.5ml/½ tsp mild chilli
powder
2.5ml/½ tsp nigella seeds,
plus a few extra to garnish
Few sprigs coriander/
cilantro, to garnish
5ml/1 tsp lemon juice
Salt and ground black
pepper

1 Mix together the cauliflower, onion, garlic, ginger, oil
and seasoning in the mug and microwave uncovered
on full power for 3 minutes.

2 Add all the other ingredients except the coriander
and lemon juice and mix thoroughly, making sure
that the ginger and garlic from the bottom of the
mug are properly combined. Cover and microwave for
2 minutes.

3 Remove the cover and then microwave again for
1 minute and stir. Leave to stand for 1 minute.

4 Garnish with sprigs of coriander, a few extra nigella
seeds and lemon juice.

CHEF'S TIPS:
This isn't meant to be a sloppy curry so it will be quite
dry; if you want more liquid just add a dash of
vegetable stock at the end.

This is a twist on Bombay potatoes which are usually
served as a side dish or part of a larger meal; I've
included the chickpeas to transform this into a whole
meal in a mug. Try it with some yogurt on the side.

If you don't have all the spices use ready-made
curry powder.

The island of Cyprus sits on the edge of the Middle East and the Mediterranean. My couscous is an amalgamation of the Cypriot flavours of zesty feta and sharp pomegranate with the warming Middle Eastern spices of cumin and paprika.

CYPRIOT COUSCOUS WITH FETA

1 Mix together the aubergine, onion, garlic, olive oil, peas, tomatoes, paprika and cumin in the mug and microwave uncovered on full power for 3 minutes.

2 Mix the couscous into the vegetables and then add the vegetable stock. Cover and microwave on full power for 1 minute and then leave to stand for 1 minute.

3 Using a fork break up the couscous and gently fold in the coriander, flaked almonds, pomegranate seeds and feta cheese. Serve garnished with a few extra sprigs of coriander.

CHEF'S TIP:
This is a really good dish to indulge in a variety of vegetables; add any combination you want but try to keep them all diced to approximately the same size so they cook evenly.

SERVES 1
COOKING TIME: **4 minutes (800W microwave), plus 1 minute standing**
EQUIPMENT: **300ml/½ pint mug**

50g/2oz aubergine/ eggplant, diced
15g/½oz onion, diced
1 clove garlic, diced
15ml/1 tbsp olive oil
30g/1¼oz frozen peas
20g/¾oz/2 cherry tomatoes, diced

2.5ml/½ tsp paprika
2.5ml/½ tsp ground cumin
60g/2¼oz couscous
100ml/3½fl oz/scant ½ cup vegetable stock
30ml/2 tbsp fresh coriander/ cilantro leaves, torn, plus a few extra sprigs to garnish
15ml/1 tbsp flaked/sliced almonds
15ml/1 tbsp pomegranate seeds
30g/1¼oz feta cheese, crumbled

A tasty dish that never fails to satisfy a case of the emergency munchies! This recipe is an ideal vegetarian mug meal for when you want something spicy, filling and quick with a slight nod to Asian flavours. The addition of egg into the dish adds some protein and creates a much heartier meal.

ORIENTAL EGG NOODLES

SERVES 1
COOKING TIME: 6½ minutes
(800W microwave)
EQUIPMENT: 500ml/17fl oz
mug, small bowl

60g/2¼oz dried egg noodles
350ml/12fl oz/1½ cups hot
   water
60g/2¼oz shiitake
   mushrooms, thinly sliced
2 spring onions/scallions,
   sliced
1 clove garlic, chopped

½ pak choi/bok choy,
   cut lengthways and roughly
   sliced
1 egg, whisked
1 red chilli, sliced
15ml/1 tbsp vegetable oil
Few sprigs fresh coriander/
   cilantro, to garnish

For the sauce:
15ml/1 tbsp soy sauce
15ml/1 tbsp nuts, chopped
7.5ml/1½ tsp sesame oil
5ml/1 tsp sesame seeds

1 Break the noodles into thirds to fit inside the mug, add all the water and microwave uncovered on full power for 4 minutes, then drain.

2 Add the mushrooms, spring onions, garlic, pak choi, egg, chilli and oil to the noodles in the mug and thoroughly combine. Microwave uncovered on full power for 2½ minutes.

3 In a small bowl mix all the sauce ingredients together and then stir through the noodle mixture. Serve garnished with sprigs of coriander.

CHEF'S TIP:
I love this dish as it stands but it makes a great base for any other ingredients you might have in your refrigerator that you want to use up.

Ratatouille is a wonderfully rich vegetarian dish, the ultimate in village food. The inclusion of puy lentils turns this recipe into a filling meal for one and a touch of turmeric and coriander gives a nice Asian slant on an otherwise French classic.

SPICED RATATOUILLE WITH PUY LENTILS

SERVES 1
COOKING TIME: 5 minutes (800W microwave), plus 1 minute standing
EQUIPMENT: 300ml/½ pint mug

15g/½oz red onion, sliced
1 clove garlic, grated
40g/1½oz aubergine/ eggplant, diced
40g/1½oz courgette/ zucchini, diced
30g/1¼oz red bell pepper, diced
30ml/2 tbsp extra virgin olive oil
1.5ml/¼ tsp turmeric
75ml/5 tbsp canned tomatoes
60ml/4 tbsp puy lentils, pre-cooked
2.5ml/½ tsp balsamic vinegar
15ml/1 tbsp chopped fresh coriander/cilantro, plus a few extra sprigs to garnish
Squeeze lemon juice
Salt and ground black pepper

1 Place the onion, garlic, aubergine, courgette, red pepper and olive oil in the mug – it will almost be overflowing with ingredients at this point, but once microwaved they will reduce in volume by almost half. Microwave uncovered on full power for 3 minutes.

2 Next add the turmeric, tomatoes, puy lentils, balsamic vinegar and seasoning and microwave uncovered on full power for 2 minutes.

3 Leave to stand for 1 minute, add the coriander and lemon juice and mix through. Season to taste before serving garnished with a few extra sprigs of coriander.

CHEF'S TIPS:
A dollop of Greek/US strained plain yogurt and a pinch of dried chilli flakes go really well!

Pre-cooked puy lentils are now available in all supermarkets, but if you don't have any available you can always replace the lentils with canned chickpeas or butter/lima beans.

A Mediterranean favourite, with earthy green lentils, zesty feta, smoky chilli flakes – I can literally feel my body thanking me for eating something so healthy! Green lentils make an excellent platform to add a variety of ingredients. This is a surprisingly filling mug meal that satisfies the most hungry of cravings.

GREEN LENTIL AND FETA SALAD

SERVES 1
COOKING TIME: 4½ minutes
  (800W microwave)
EQUIPMENT: 500ml/17fl oz
mug, small bowl

25g/1oz red onion,
  3 quarters finely diced,
  1 quarter finely sliced
1 clove garlic, finely sliced
40g/1½oz potato, diced
30ml/2 tbsp extra virgin
  olive oil
100g/3¾oz canned green
  lentils, drained and rinsed

15ml/1 tbsp water
40g/1½oz/about 4 cherry
  tomatoes, diced
20g/¾oz baby spinach,
  roughly sliced
Pinch dried oregano
2.5ml/½ tsp vinegar
30ml/2 tbsp chopped fresh
  parsley
30g/1¼oz feta cheese,
  crumbled
Pinch chilli flakes
Salt and ground black
  pepper

1 Combine the diced onion, garlic, potato and half the olive oil in the mug and microwave uncovered on full power for 3 minutes.

2 Add the lentils and water and microwave covered for a further 90 seconds. Drain away any excess liquid.

3 Gently stir through the sliced onion, tomatoes, spinach, oregano, vinegar, parsley and remaining oil. Top with the feta cheese and chilli flakes, and season to taste.

CHEF'S TIP:
Try swapping the vinegar for lemon juice and the parsley for fresh mint for a slightly different direction of flavour.

A classic American favourite that has become somewhat of an institution. Loved the world over as one of the ultimate comfort foods, the humble Mac'n'Cheese can be found in a can or as gourmet street food. My version is cooked in minutes, and it goes great with a bad film on the sofa!

MAC & CHEESE

SERVES 1
COOKING TIME: **9 minutes**
 (800W microwave)
EQUIPMENT: **500ml/17fl oz**
 mug, bowl

80g/3¼oz/½ cup dried
 macaroni
250ml/8fl oz/1 cup hot water
Pinch salt
15ml/1 tbsp butter

15ml/1 tbsp flour
100ml/3½fl oz/scant ½ cup
 milk
2.5ml/½ tsp mustard, ideally
 English
50g/2oz grated Cheddar
 cheese, use mature/sharp
 for extra cheesy flavour!
Salt and ground black
 pepper

1 Add the macaroni, water and salt to a bowl and microwave uncovered on full power for 7 minutes, drain and set aside.

2 Melt the butter in the mug in the microwave for 30 seconds, then add the flour and mix thoroughly.

3 Adding a few drops of milk at a time, mix the butter, flour and milk into a paste with a fork before adding the rest of the milk all at once.

4 Microwave uncovered on full power for 30 seconds, remove and whisk thoroughly with a fork. It will be lumpy, sticky and basically a mess but all will change in literally a minute.

5 Microwave again for just under 1 minute (about 55 seconds) and then add the mustard and cheese and season to taste.

6 Pour the macaroni into your cheese sauce and stir well.

CHEF'S TIPS:
Try using different cheeses for different flavours or a combination of cheeses such as a Stilton and Cheddar.
It's not vegetarian but if you like you could cook a rasher/strip of bacon until really crispy and crumble on top of the Mac & Cheese for a little crunch!

If a Mac & Cheese is an American institution this a Greek's homemade version. I remember eating this as a kid when my mum needed to get something on the table super-quick to stop a frenzy of hungry children going crazy! This is a family favourite, simple, delicious and great for kids and adults.

GREEK MAC & CHEESE

1 Add the macaroni, water and salt to the mug and microwave uncovered on full power for 7 minutes.

2 Drain the pasta and immediately add the grated Halloumi cheese, mint and butter and mix well. Season to taste and serve.

CHEF'S TIP:
Try adding a little crumbled feta cheese at the end to garnish and give another dimension to the dish!

SERVES 1
COOKING TIME: 7 minutes
(800W microwave)
EQUIPMENT: 500ml/17fl oz
mug

80g/3¼oz/½ cup macaroni
250ml/8fl oz/1 cup hot water

Pinch salt
15g/½oz grated Halloumi
cheese
2.5ml/½ tsp dried mint
7.5ml/1½ tsp butter
Salt and ground black
pepper

SOMETHING SWEET TO FINISH

Baking mug cakes in the microwave has proved hugely popular and is a wonderful way of getting your sweet fix in literally a matter of minutes. The great thing about microwave mug cakes is that many have the same basic cake mixture, meaning you can play with the flavour combinations. I've also found that adding ground almonds to a cake makes it a slightly more dense and moist cake than using just flour, giving rise (excuse the pun) to you also being able to play with the consistency you prefer. However, it's not all about cakes. The microwave is a great way of whipping up some lovely alternative sweet-tooth recipes, including my Greek-inspired, fragrant rice pudding.

Greek rice pudding or rizogalo – in Greek translated as ryzi (rice) and galo (mik) – is equally at home served warm as a comforting winter dessert or straight from the refrigerator for something refreshing in the hot sun. But don't be fooled by this humble dish; it is velvety and utterly satisfying.

RIZOGALO – GREEK RICE PUDDING

SERVES 1
COOKING TIME: 13–14
  minutes (800W
  microwave), plus
  2 minutes standing
EQUIPMENT: 500ml/17fl oz
  mug

40g/1½oz Arborio rice
180ml/6¼fl oz/generous ¾
  cup water
45ml/3 tbsp full-fat/whole
  milk
15ml/1 tbsp butter
25ml/1½ tbsp sugar
Few drops vanilla extract
Pinch ground cinnamon and
  chopped pistachio nuts,
  to garnish

1 Place the rice and water in the mug and microwave uncovered on full power for 5 minutes – be sure to place on a microwaveproof plate to catch any overspill of water.

2 Remove from the microwave, stir and then leave to stand for 1 minute. Then, return to the microwave and cook uncovered for a further 4 minutes.

3 Add the milk, butter, sugar and vanilla extract, combine thoroughly and microwave for 4 minutes. Leave to stand for a further 1 minute.

4 At this stage the rice pudding has a lovely al dente texture, however if you prefer a softer texture add a dash of milk and microwave for a further 30 seconds to 1 minute.

5 When you are satisfied with the texture of the rice garnish with cinnamon and pistachio nuts and enjoy!

CHEF'S TIPS:
Using Arborio rice means the more time you spend stirring the rice the more starch it will release and create a creamier dessert. The benefit of this is you don't need to add any cream, eggs or cornflour, you could even omit the butter if preferred (but I like a bit of butter to create a slighter richer taste!).
   You can use any fat content of milk you have, the higher the fat/cream content the richer the rice pudding will be.

I first encountered 'chai' whilst travelling through India. For a couple of rupees a Chaiwala (a street tea seller) will extravagantly pour you a small cup of well-brewed tea. Traditionally, chai should be infused with a variety of whole spices and be heady with the fragrance of cloves, cinnamon and cardamom.

AFTERNOON CHAI CAKE

SERVES 1
COOKING TIME: 2¼ minutes
  (800W microwave), plus
  1 minute standing
EQUIPMENT: bowl, 300ml/
  ½ pint mug

75ml/5 tbsp milk
1 chai teabag
40g/1½oz plain/all-purpose
  flour
15ml/1 tbsp caster/superfine
  sugar
2.5ml/½ tsp baking powder
15ml/1 tbsp vegetable oil
Few drops vanilla extract
15ml/1 tbsp strawberry jam
15ml/1 tbsp clotted or
  whipped cream,
  to serve

1 Heat the milk in a bowl for 45 seconds or until just boiling and add the chai teabag. Leave this to steep while you prepare the rest of the muffin, giving it a stir every now and again to help it infuse the milk.

2 Place the flour, sugar and baking powder into a clean mug and combine thoroughly.

3 Add the oil, vanilla extract and 60ml/4 tbsp of the infused milk to the dry ingredients in the mug. Stir to combine but don't over-mix, a few lumps are alright.

4 Carefully add the jam to the centre of the mixture and let it sit, don't stir. Microwave uncovered on full power for 1½ minutes.

5 Leave it to stand for 1 minute before adding the clotted cream to the top and serving immediately.

CHEF'S TIP:
Try making your own chai by infusing regular black tea with whole spices such as cinnamon, cloves, ginger, cardamom and sugar.

There is nothing quite like a good chocolate cake and this one offers a little something extra. I'm not normally a fan of chocolate orange but I like the use of marmalade which gives a subtle depth of flavour that isn't overpowering while the ground almonds keep the cake nice and moist.

CHOCOLATE ORANGE CAKE

1 Place the egg, oil, milk, orange zest, salt and marmalade in the mug and whisk with a fork until fully combined.

2 Add the rest of the ingredients and combine thoroughly.

3 Microwave uncovered on full power for 1½ minutes and leave to stand for 2 minutes. Serve with a dollop of whipped cream if you like!

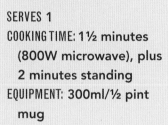

SERVES 1
COOKING TIME: 1½ minutes (800W microwave), plus 2 minutes standing
EQUIPMENT: 300ml/½ pint mug

1 small/US medium egg
30ml/2 tbsp vegetable oil
45ml/3 tbsp milk
15ml/1 tbsp orange zest
Good pinch salt
30ml/2 tbsp marmalade

30ml/2 tbsp plain/all-purpose flour
15ml/1 tbsp ground almonds
15ml/1 tbsp caster/superfine sugar
45ml/3 tbsp cocoa powder
2.5ml/½ tsp baking powder
10g/¼oz dark chocolate (85% cocoa solids), broken up into small pieces
Whipped cream, to serve (optional)

CHEF'S TIPS:
The broken chocolate creates little pockets of lovely melted chocolate.
I like my cake to be just cooked so still gooey; if you want it well done, cook for 2 minutes.
If you use too much marmalade it will change the consistency, so don't get greedy!

These are two of my favourite ingredients – big ripe juicy blueberries and almonds – a perfect combination. For me this is a truly indulgent bake, I love how the cooking of the blueberries concentrates their sweetness and they burst across the cake like street graffiti, and the almonds add a crunch – enjoy at your peril!

BLUEBERRY AND ALMOND CAKE

SERVES 1
COOKING TIME: 2½ minutes (800W microwave), plus 1 minute standing
EQUIPMENT: 300ml/½ pint mug

60ml/4 tbsp plain/all-purpose flour
15ml/1 tbsp ground almonds
15ml/1 tbsp flaked/sliced almonds, plus 15ml/1 tbsp to garnish
15ml/1 tbsp caster/superfine sugar
1.5ml/¼ tsp baking powder
Pinch salt
1 egg yolk
25ml/1½ tbsp vegetable oil
45ml/3 tbsp milk
Few drops vanilla extract
35g/1⅓oz blueberries

1 Place the flour, almonds (ground and flaked), sugar, baking powder and salt in the mug and combine thoroughly.

2 Next add the egg yolk, oil, milk and vanilla extract and whisk until fully incorporated.

3 Fold in the blueberries, scatter the remaining 15ml/1 tbsp flaked almonds on top and microwave uncovered on full power for 2½ minutes. Leave to stand for 1 minute before devouring.

CHEF'S TIP:
Try adding other fruits; blackcurrants or raspberries are also delicious!

Let's just take a moment: sweet caramel maple syrup, crunchy pecan nuts, moist bananas – does it get any better? Those three ingredients are like the holy trinity of an indulgent dessert. This is the perfect moist and rich muffin for when you want a quick guilty fix of something naughty to eat!

BANANA MUFFIN WITH PECAN AND MAPLE SYRUP

SERVES 1
COOKING TIME: 1¾ minutes (800W microwave), plus 1 minute standing
EQUIPMENT: 300ml/½ pint mug

1 small/US medium egg
7.5ml/1½ tsp oil
15ml/1 tbsp maple syrup
30ml/2 tbsp milk
60g/2¼oz/about ½ ripe banana, mashed

40g/1½oz plain/all-purpose flour
5ml/1 tsp baking powder
2.5ml/½ tsp ground cinnamon
Few drops vanilla extract
7.5ml/1½ tsp sugar
10g/¼oz crushed pecan nuts, plus a few extra to garnish

1 Place the egg, oil, maple syrup and milk in the mug and whisk together.

2 Then add all the other ingredients, except the pecan nuts to garnish, and combine.

3 Sprinkle a few extra pecan nuts on top and microwave uncovered on full power for 1¾ minutes.

4 Leave to stand for 1 minute before eating!

NUTRITIONAL INFORMATION

PASTA (serves 1) Energy 205kcal/874kJ; Protein 7.2g; Carbohydrate 44.5g, of which sugars 2g; Fat 1.1g, of which saturates 0.1g; Cholesterol 0mg; Calcium 15mg; Fibre 2.3g; Sodium 2mg.

MASH (serves 1) Energy 161kcal/676kJ; Protein 2.6g; Carbohydrate 24.2g, of which sugars 2g; Fat 6.6g, of which saturates 4.1g; Cholesterol 66mg; Calcium 10mg; Fibre 2g; Sodium 62mg.

RICE (serves 1) Energy 180kcal/751kJ; Protein 3.7g; Carbohydrate 39.9g, of which sugars 0g; Fat 0.2g, of which saturates 0g; Cholesterol 0mg; Calcium 10mg; Fibre 0g; Sodium 0mg.

ALL-DAY BREAKFAST (serves 1) Energy 514kcal/2128kJ; Protein 17.1g; Carbohydrate 10g, of which sugars 2.6g; Fat 45.3g, of which saturates 10g; Cholesterol 288mg; Calcium 60mg; Fibre 1.2g; Sodium 748mg.

RAPIDO HUEVOS RANCHEROS (serves 1) Energy 343kcal/1420kJ; Protein 10.9g; Carbohydrate 9.3g, of which sugars 8.4g; Fat 29.4g, of which saturates 5.1g; Cholesterol 231mg; Calcium 130mg; Fibre 3.3g; Sodium 177mg.

MAGIC EGGS FLORENTINE (serves 1) Energy 759kcal/3147kJ; Protein 18g; Carbohydrate 32.2g, of which sugars 2.8g; Fat 62.9g, of which saturates 35g; Cholesterol 561mg; Calcium 157mg; Fibre 1.9g; Sodium 767mg.

PUFFIN IN A MUG (serves 1) Energy 406kcal/1709kJ; Protein 21.3g; Carbohydrate 50g, of which sugars 2.8g; Fat 14.8g, of which saturates 6.5g; Cholesterol 254mg; Calcium 382mg; Fibre 2.6g; Sodium 839mg.

SPEEDY SPAGHETTI BOLOGNESE (serves 1) Energy 535kcal/2240kJ; Protein 26.6g; Carbohydrate 49g, of which sugars 5.9g; Fat 27.2g, of which saturates 9.1g; Cholesterol 53mg; Calcium 187mg; Fibre 3.5g; Sodium 205mg.

VIETNAMESE-STYLE BEEF PHO (serves 1) Energy 402kcal/1677kJ; Protein 16.7g; Carbohydrate 55.2g, of which sugars 2.9g; Fat 11.9g, of which saturates 1.9g; Cholesterol 20mg; Calcium 292mg; Fibre 3.4g; Sodium 890mg.

CHILLI CON CARNE WITH RICE (serves 1) Energy 383kcal/1602kJ; Protein 26.3g; Carbohydrate 43g, of which sugars 7.8g; Fat 16.3g, of which saturates 4.9g; Cholesterol 39mg; Calcium 341mg; Fibre 9.3g; Sodium 826mg.

FUSS-FREE BEEF STIFADO (serves 1) Energy 603kcal/2499kJ; Protein 24.8g; Carbohydrate 18.9g, of which sugars 5.3g; Fat 48g, of which saturates 7.8g; Cholesterol 46mg; Calcium 38mg; Fibre 7.5g; Sodium 473mg.

STUFFED RED PEPPER WITH FETA CHEESE (serves 1) Energy 311kcal/1294kJ; Protein 15.2g; Carbohydrate 22g, of which sugars 13.6g; Fat 18.5g, of which saturates 7.3g; Cholesterol 39mg; Calcium 209mg; Fibre 7.1g; Sodium 478mg.

LAMB 'TAGINE' IN A MUG (serves 1) Energy 719kcal/2996kJ; Protein 30g; Carbohydrate 38.9g, of which sugars 22.3g; Fat 51.9g, of which saturates 8.7g; Cholesterol 59mg; Calcium 484mg; Fibre 9.1g; Sodium 326mg.

'GET YOUR JERK ON' SHEPHERD'S PIE (serves 1) Energy 447kcal/1874kJ; Protein 18g; Carbohydrate 51.4g, of which sugars 17.1g; Fat 20.3g, of which saturates 8.1g; Cholesterol 62mg; Calcium 73mg; Fibre 9g; Sodium 1114mg.

TOWERING MOUSSAKA (serves 1) Energy 626kcal/2602kJ; Protein 32.1g; Carbohydrate 19g, of which sugars 7.2g; Fat 47.4g, of which saturates 25g; Cholesterol 140mg; Calcium 564mg; Fibre 3.4g; Sodium 551mg.

LAMB SATAY CURRY (serves 1) Energy 504kcal/2099kJ; Protein 24.2g; Carbohydrate 36.1g, of which sugars 12.8g; Fat 29.3g, of which saturates 7.4g; Cholesterol 52mg; Calcium 76mg; Fibre 1.8g; Sodium 803mg.

LEMON AND OREGANO LAMB STEW (serves 1) Energy 530kcal/2205kJ; Protein 24.5g; Carbohydrate 28.2g, of which sugars 3.1g; Fat 36.3g, of which saturates 9.6g; Cholesterol 87mg; Calcium 65mg; Fibre 4.1g; Sodium 75mg.

FEIJOADA – BRAZILIAN BLACK BEAN STEW (serves 1) Energy 611kcal/2544kJ; Protein 27.9g; Carbohydrate 35.4g, of which sugars 7.6g; Fat 40.8g, of which saturates 9.5g; Cholesterol 55mg; Calcium 147mg; Fibre 15.3g; Sodium 1064mg.

THE BIG EASY – LOUISIANA GUMBO (serves 1) Energy 573kcal/2393kJ; Protein 21.2g; Carbohydrate 39.5g, of which sugars 7.7g; Fat 37.9g, of which saturates 7.9g; Cholesterol 93mg; Calcium 145mg; Fibre 7.5g; Sodium 908mg.

HONG KONG CLAY HOTPOT RICE (serves 1) Energy 527kcal/2190kJ; Protein 22g; Carbohydrate 35.1g, of which sugars 2.9g; Fat 33.1g, of which saturates 8.8g; Cholesterol 65mg; Calcium 30mg; Fibre 2g; Sodium 1146mg.

LAAP – A LAOS NATIONAL DISH (serves 1) Energy 324kcal/1352kJ; Protein 18.2g; Carbohydrate 19.6g, of which sugars 2.2g; Fat 19.5g, of which saturates 4.2g; Cholesterol 53mg; Calcium 112mg; Fibre 3.3g; Sodium 1143mg.

PORK BELLY DHAL (Serves 1) Energy 477kcal/1994kJ; Protein 26.4g; Carbohydrate 34.7g, of which sugars 2.2g; Fat 27.2g, of which saturates 12.6g; Cholesterol 74mg; Calcium 67mg; Fibre 3.9g; Sodium 753mg.

FIERY AUBERGINE WITH PORK IN SOY (serves 1) Energy 191kcal/801kJ; Protein 12.4g; Carbohydrate 12.4g, of which sugars 12g; Fat 10.6g, of which saturates 2.7g; Cholesterol 33mg; Calcium 33mg; Fibre 4.2g; Sodium 1111mg.

SURPRISINGLY AUTHENTIC SPAGHETTI CARBONARA (serves 1) Energy 568kcal/2383kJ; Protein 27.9g; Carbohydrate 59.8g, of which sugars 3.1g; Fat 25.7g, of which saturates 9.5g; Cholesterol 255mg; Calcium 231mg; Fibre 4.1g; Sodium 886mg.

STUFFED CHICKEN BREAST WITH CHICKPEAS (serves 1) Energy 512kcal/2130kJ; Protein 34.4g; Carbohydrate 10.8g, of which sugars 2.7g; Fat 37.1g, of which saturates 13.7g; Cholesterol 118mg; Calcium 81mg; Fibre 4.3g; Sodium 1123mg.

CHORIZO, LENTIL AND GOAT'S CHEESE (serves 1) Energy 476kcal/1977kJ; Protein 20.3g; Carbohydrate 17.7g, of which sugars 5.1g; Fat 36.5g, of which saturates 12g; Cholesterol 28mg; Calcium 126mg; Fibre 8.9g; Sodium 371mg.

MEXICAN CHICKEN AND CHIPOTLE (serves 1) Energy 397kcal/1659kJ; Protein 27.9g; Carbohydrate 17g, of which sugars 4.9g; Fat 24.7g, of which saturates 3.6g; Cholesterol 70mg; Calcium 19mg; Fibre 2.8g; Sodium 100mg.

WARM ORZO AND LEMON CHICKEN (serves 1) Energy 306kcal/1276kJ; Protein 22.6g; Carbohydrate 25.7g, of which sugars 1.8g; Fat 12.3g, of which saturates 1.9g; Cholesterol 56mg; Calcium 26mg; Fibre 1g; Sodium 52mg.

QUICK CHICKEN BIRYANI (serves 1) Energy 640kcal/2665kJ; Protein 31.6g; Carbohydrate 46.7g, of which sugars 9.4g; Fat 36.8g, of which saturates 7.5g; Cholesterol 86mg; Calcium 74mg; Fibre 0.9g; Sodium 708mg.

HELLENIC CHICKEN AND LEMON RISOTTO (serves 1) Energy 500kcal/2087kJ; Protein 34.1g; Carbohydrate 47.6g, of which sugars 2.2g; Fat 19.1g, of which saturates 6.2g; Cholesterol 84mg; Calcium 197mg; Fibre 2.8g; Sodium 491mg.

MEDITERRANEAN COD ON AUBERGINE (serves 1) Energy 183kcal/760kJ; Protein 17.1g; Carbohydrate 1.9g, of which sugars 1.8g; Fat 11.9g, of which saturates 1.7g; Cholesterol 41mg; Calcium 15mg; Fibre 1.7g; Sodium 57mg.

SMOKED HADDOCK CHOWDER (serves 1) Energy 295kcal/1237kJ; Protein 19.5g; Carbohydrate 23.6g, of which sugars 6.6g; Fat 14.3g, of which saturates 8.5g; Cholesterol 90mg; Calcium 106mg; Fibre 2.6g; Sodium 816mg.

SEAFOOD PAELLA (serves 1) Energy 467kcal/1954kJ; Protein 36.8g; Carbohydrate 46.7g, of which sugars 1.6g; Fat 14.9g, of which saturates 2.3g; Cholesterol 401mg; Calcium 118mg; Fibre 0.8g; Sodium 286mg.

CURRIED FISH PIE (serves 1) Energy 462kcal/1940kJ; Protein 43.7g; Carbohydrate 36.2g, of which sugars 7.3g; Fat 16.9g, of which saturates 9.5g; Cholesterol 240mg; Calcium 256mg; Fibre 8g; Sodium 1069mg.

STEAMED GINGER SEABASS ON NOODLES (serves 1) Energy 333kcal/1401kJ; Protein 21.2g; Carbohydrate 39g, of which sugars 4g; Fat 11.3g, of which saturates 2.2g; Cholesterol 71mg; Calcium 192mg; Fibre 3.4g; Sodium 565mg.

ASIAN COCONUT SOUP (serves1) Energy 187kcal/784kJ; Protein 21.7g; Carbohydrate 9.2g, of which sugars 8.9g; Fat 7.2g, of which saturates 1g; Cholesterol 195mg; Calcium 313mg; Fibre 5.6g; Sodium 417mg.

CHILLI SALMON AND SPINACH SALAD (serves 1) Energy 436kcal/1803kJ; Protein 21.6g; Carbohydrate 1.3g, of which sugars 1.1g; Fat 38.3g, of which saturates 5.8g; Cholesterol 50mg; Calcium 91mg; Fibre 1.1g; Sodium 635mg.

STOLEN KISS SEAFOOD PASTA (serves 1) Energy 667kcal/2792kJ; Protein 28.5g; Carbohydrate 62g, of which sugars 5.2g; Fat 35.6g, of which saturates 5g; Cholesterol 195mg; Calcium 163mg; Fibre 5.9g; Sodium 208mg.

SQUID INK RISOTTO (serves 1) Energy 530kcal/2201kJ; Protein 14.4g; Carbohydrate 50.6g, of which sugars 1.5g; Fat 29.7g, of which saturates 7.3g; Cholesterol 151mg; Calcium 56mg; Fibre 1.4g; Sodium 117mg.

PROVENÇAL PEAS & SALMON (serves 1) Energy 594kcal/2454kJ; Protein 27.4g; Carbohydrate 23.4g, of which sugars 4.8g; Fat 44.1g, of which saturates 6.6g; Cholesterol 45mg; Calcium 62mg; Fibre 7.7g; Sodium 550mg.

PAP'S MAGIC MUSSELS (serves 1) Energy 341kcal/1413kJ; Protein 14.5g; Carbohydrate 3.6g, of which sugars 0.8g; Fat 29.8g, of which saturates 10.3g; Cholesterol 80mg; Calcium 105mg; Fibre 2g; Sodium 389mg.

DECADENT MUSHROOM RISOTTO WITH PINE NUTS (serves 1) Energy 464kcal/1926kJ; Protein 10.5g; Carbohydrate 41.2g, of which sugars 1.1g; Fat 27.1g, of which saturates 8.7g; Cholesterol 30mg; Calcium 169mg; Fibre 0.5g; Sodium 160mg.

WHITE BEAN AND CITRUS CASSOULET (serves 1) Energy 326kcal/1355kJ; Protein 8g; Carbohydrate 23.1g, of which sugars 8.1g; Fat 23g, of which saturates 3.3g; Cholesterol 0mg; Calcium 94mg; Fibre 10.5g; Sodium 898mg.

BOMBAY CAULIFLOWER (serves 1) Energy 207kcal/865kJ; Protein 10.2g; Carbohydrate 20.3g, of which sugars 5.2g; Fat 10.4g, of which saturates 4.6g; Cholesterol 16mg; Calcium 77mg; Fibre 6.4g; Sodium 168mg.

CYPRIOT COUSCOUS WITH FETA (serves 1) Energy 318kcal/1323kJ; Protein 12g; Carbohydrate 34.9g, of which sugars 3.2g; Fat 15.3g, of which saturates 4.8g; Cholesterol 21mg; Calcium 165mg; Fibre 1.7g; Sodium 436mg.

ORIENTAL EGG NOODLES (serves 1) Energy 621kcal/2593kJ; Protein 23.6g; Carbohydrate 48.2g, of which sugars 5g; Fat 38.4g, of which saturates 7.3g; Cholesterol 249mg; Calcium 235mg; Fibre 6.2g; Sodium 1371mg.

SPICED RATATOUILLE WITH PUY LENTILS (serves 1) Energy 289kcal/1202kJ; Protein 7g; Carbohydrate 14.9g, of which sugars 4.3g; Fat 22.9g, of which saturates 3.2g; Cholesterol 0mg; Calcium 60mg; Fibre 6.1g; Sodium 37mg.

GREEN LENTIL AND FETA SALAD (serves 1) Energy 437kcal/1819kJ; Protein 16.2g; Carbohydrate 28.1g, of which sugars 5g; Fat 29.6g, of which saturates 7.5g; Cholesterol 34mg; Calcium 235mg; Fibre 9.2g; Sodium 482mg.

MAC & CHEESE (serves 1) Energy 579kcal/2439kJ; Protein 27g; Carbohydrate 75.9g, of which sugars 7.8g; Fat 20.7g, of which saturates 12.1g; Cholesterol 56mg; Calcium 520mg; Fibre 3.7g; Sodium 414mg.

GREEK MAC & CHEESE (serves 1) Energy 367kcal/1550kJ; Protein 12g; Carbohydrate 59.6g, of which sugars 2.9g; Fat 10.6g, of which saturates 6.1g; Cholesterol 27mg; Calcium 75mg; Fibre 3.1g; Sodium 264mg.

RIZOGALO – GREEK RICE PUDDING (serves 1) Energy 366kcal/1531kJ; Protein 4.6g; Carbohydrate 56.9g, of which sugars 24.9g; Fat 14.3g, of which saturates 8.9g; Cholesterol 38mg; Calcium 76mg; Fibre 0g; Sodium 117mg.

AFTERNOON CHAI CAKE (serves 1) Energy 372kcal/1569kJ; Protein 6.5g; Carbohydrate 61.7g, of which sugars 30.3g; Fat 12.7g, of which saturates 2.2g; Cholesterol 5mg; Calcium 173mg; Fibre 1.7g; Sodium 339mg.

CHOCOLATE ORANGE CAKE (serves 1) Energy 754kcal/3152kJ; Protein 17.7g; Carbohydrate 77.1g, of which sugars 44g; Fat 43.7g, of which saturates 9g; Cholesterol 212mg; Calcium 162mg; Fibre 5g; Sodium 272mg.

BLUEBERRY AND ALMOND CAKE (serves 1) Energy 693kcal/2897kJ; Protein 16.4g; Carbohydrate 71.8g, of which sugars 23.7g; Fat 39.8g, of which saturates 5.4g; Cholesterol 205mg; Calcium 233mg; Fibre 3.6g; Sodium 39mg.

BANANA MUFFIN WITH PECAN AND MAPLE SYRUP (serves 1) Energy 490kcal/2056kJ; Protein 13.6g; Carbohydrate 66.9g, of which sugars 32g; Fat 20.4g, of which saturates 3.5g; Cholesterol 214mg; Calcium 199mg; Fibre 3.2g; Sodium 686mg.

INDEX

CREDITS

This edition is published by Lorenz Books, an imprint of Anness Publishing Ltd, 108 Great Russell Street, London WC1B 3NA; info@anness.com

www.lorenzbooks.com; www.annesspublishing.com; twitter: @Anness_Books

If you like the images in this book and would like to investigate using them for publishing, promotions or advertising, please visit our website www.practicalpictures.com for more information.

© Anness Publishing Ltd 2016

Publisher: Joanna Lorenz
Photography: William Shaw
Food styling: Emma Frost
Prop styling: Pene Parker
Design: Adelle Mahoney
Editorial: Sarah Lumby
Production controller: Pirong Wang

PUBLISHER'S NOTE
Although the advice and information in this book are believed to be accurate and true at the time of going to press, neither the authors nor the publisher can accept any legal responsibility or liability for any errors or omissions that may have been made nor for any inaccuracies nor for any loss, harm or injury that comes about from following instructions or advice in this book. Always refer to your microwave's handbook for usage advice.

COOK'S NOTES
For all recipes, quantities are given in both metric and imperial measures and, where appropriate, in standard cups and spoons. Follow one set of measures, but not a mixture, because they are not interchangeable. Standard spoon and cup measures are level. 1 tsp = 5ml, 1 tbsp = 15ml, 1 cup = 250ml/8fl oz. Australian standard tablespoons are 20ml. Australian readers should use 3 tsp in place of 1 tbsp for measuring small quantities. American pints are 16fl oz/2 cups. American readers should use 20fl oz/2.5 cups in place of 1 pint when measuring liquids. Medium (US large) eggs are used unless otherwise stated.